WISBOROUGHS

TIME FOR A FRESH VIEW ON LIFE

An Easy Way to Personal Development
by
Learning from Everything You Do

Chrissie McGinn & Richard Hewitt

Published in the UK 1995

Copyright Chrissie McGinn & Richard Hewitt

ISBN 09516963 9 4

Published by

Wessex Aquarian Publications
P.O. Box 1059
Sturminster Newton
Dorset
DT10 1YA
England

Printed in Great Britain by Intype, London.

For the families we chose
so that we could learn so much
with love

ACKNOWLEDGEMENTS

Our thanks to Gill Edwards for writing a book which set us on our new path and gave us the belief that we could write this book. We were also inspired by the work of Alistair Mant, John Bradshaw, Alan Mumford, and the Friels. Andy and Annette Lawson's invitation to go to Australia also pushed us in the right direction.

It was only with Gerald Batt, David Goodwin and Ian Cunningham's encouragement during the first draft, that we continued to work towards publication.

Thanks to Josephine Sellers for her belief that the book should be published.

Finally, we coudn't have written this book without our clients, both as individuals and as part of organisations. Many thanks.

FOREWORD

Unlike most books of its type which tend to be formulaic and theoretical, "Wisboroughs" is practical, sensible and well written. It is informative, instructive and most importantly - gentle. It helps the reader use their own creative resources, to review and solve life problems, be they in work, home, or other settings. I would recommend this book to anyone who is searching for intelligent and sensitive prompting in their journey through life's puzzles and dilemmas. "Wisboroughs" is an ally and source of wisdom which can only aid the search for a more rewarding and better relationship with self and others.

David Stafford

Psychoanalytic psychotherapist
Co-author of "Co-dependency"
Author of "Children of Alcoholics"
Co-Founder of the National Association
      for Children of Alcoholics

ABOUT THE AUTHORS

Over the last ten years Chrissie and Richard have worked together in a variety of settings; in organisations, with individuals and with couples.

Chrissie has an MA in Manpower Studies and trained as a Marriage Guidance counsellor ten years ago. She has been a trainer for Birmingham Social Services, a lecturer in organisational behaviour, employee development and social work management and worked in industrial relations. She has run her own consultancy, counselling and personal development business since 1986.

Richard previously worked as a lecturer in Applied Social Studies. Before that he was a training advisor, specialising in management development, although he originally trained as a teacher following his geography degree.

Chrissie and Richard have lived together for five years and worked with the usual issues that couples in second time around relationships face. By re-viewing regularly they have been able to discover new depths within themselves and their relationship. They live in Wisborough Cottage, Storrington, West Sussex, where they run many of their Wisborough programmes and personal development holidays.

CONTENTS

INTRODUCTION

Wis - to know
Wisborough - a dry safe place in a marsh

When is the right time to pick up a book? Do you find that you tend to choose a book just when you (or your organisation) need it? You might even have picked up this book before, and put it down again. The time wasn't right.

So, perhaps it isn't a coincidence that you have picked up "Wisboroughs" now. Perhaps the time is right. People often come to Wisboroughs when the time is right.

A Wisborough is a way to:
- ask yourself what you do in various situations
- identify your feelings
- think about why you behave in certain ways
- decide how you would like to be different
- change your view of yourself and your world so that you can fulfill your potential
- follow through your plan

Wisborough is a good shorthand name for this process.

Why "Wisborough"?

We chose the word Wisborough to describe our re-view and development process for several reasons. We live and work in Wisborough Cottage, and we discovered that people simply wrote "Wisborough" in their diaries on the days they were coming to our workshops. We later discovered that the word came from Wisborough Green which The Place Names of Sussex defines as probably a "hill" by the "wish" or "damp meadow". In other words, a dry safe place in a marsh. We also discovered that the word "Wis" means "to know" and comes from the same source as wise and wizard.

So, we thought that Wisborough seemed a highly appropriate word to use to describe the process you can use to help you safely discover what you want to be and how to get there.

The book will help you think about your feelings, as well as your actions, both at home and at work. In fact, it will help you see yourself, and your life, as a whole, so that you can develop as a whole person.

Origins of Wisboroughs

We originally decided to write this book as, over the years, many of our clients had suggested we should write up our work as management consultants and trainers. They found our way of working helpful, and believed others would too. Trainers thought that our methods would be useful for group faciliators to use.

At that time, most of our clients were large organisations, employing mostly men. Managers had to attend our management development courses. These managers were not interested in self development.

But, they discovered personal development on our programmes. Until then it had not occurred to them to do such work. They realised that their own personal development helped their organisations to develop.

They took what they learned on our programmes home with them. They talked to their wives about their learning, and they found that their relationships at home improved.

A personal development book was needed which men could buy because it was about work, but which they could also use at home. We knew many women who also compartmentalised their lives in a similar way and would find the book useful.

You need more than just skills!

When teaching management skills, we found it useful to look at what people <u>actually</u> did in the workplace everyday . We asked them to describe their behaviour, thoughts and feelings during specific incidents. We found that the way they would like to perform at work, and the way they performed on courses, was different from their behaviour in the workplace.

So, instead of suggesting what they could do, we looked at what was stopping them doing what they wanted to do. We found ourselves helping <u>them</u> work out how they could improve. We helped them plan how to put this into practise back at the workplace.

Lack of confidence

We often found that people were coming on courses to learn skills which they already had, but were not using because of their own lack of confidence and the constraints of the organisation. People tended to set their own limitations and allowed the organisation to reinforce them. We found that once people had set themselves free from these, they could do much more than they previously thought possible.

When we are asked to describe why our courses were different from other management skills courses we use the example of a hot air balloon. "Traditional" skills courses give information and practise and inflate the delegates with the motivation to rise from the ground like hot air balloons. They leave the course, not only walking on air but feeling full of hot air. However, once the air starts cooling on their return to the workplace, they drop to the ground again, unable to use what they have learned. No one has thought to throw out any of the ballast which was keeping them on the ground in the first place.

Our courses tended to look at the ballast and throw it out so that people could rise themselves. Throwing out the ballast helped people deal with their personal or organisational constraints.

For instance, you may believe that you

- cannot ask your boss a question because you think that you are too junior,
- are not able to speak at a meeting because you don't think people will listen to you,
- cannot ask your husband to collect the children from school because you think that men don't do such tasks.

To be able to ask or speak in any of these situations you have to free yourself from your own constraints. To release you from your constrained view, you could:

- explore why you believe a junior person can't ask a senior person a question,
- collect evidence to show how much people listen to you at meetings,
- work out where your beliefs about men and husbands come from, and check these out with your husband.

Having, in this way, cleared the ballast you can now learn the skills and apply them successfully without crashing to the ground.

The right time to learn

People often arrived on our courses to learn skills and deal with issues which were not important to them at the time. For instance, they came to learn how to do recruitment and selection interviews, although they were unlikely to be in a position to do such interviews, for another six months. What they really wanted to deal with was their current problem, e.g. their relationship with a particular supervisor or their boss. This was much more relevant to the achievement of their current objectives.

From this, we realised that some people could not learn from the course because the timing was not right for them. We began to realise the importance of helping managers achieve and learn from the work they were actually doing each day. This meant using whatever issues people brought with them to courses. This was difficult to do if the organisation wanted very specific skills taught at a specific time. This is not to say that skills training is not important; we are just highlighting the need for the right approach at the right time.

Happier lives

By this time we had discovered that the review and development process we were using, was helping us to develop our own relationship. We realised that we could help other couples develop their relationships too. Issues could be resolved with a Wisborough.

Today, our main reason for writing this book is personal. Wisboroughs can help you have a happier, healthier life, as they can help you be true to yourself; wherever you are - at work or at home.

The aim of "Wisboroughs - Make a New Start With a Fresh View on Life" is to help you re-view your everyday experiences so that you can become aware of the choices available to you, and develop in any way you wish. Perhaps by behaving differently, seeing the world another way, creating your own values and beliefs, valuing yourself, or becoming more soulful. Who knows how much you will discover as you begin to choose.

HOW TO USE THIS BOOK

"WISBOROUGHS - Make a New Start With a Fresh View on Life" is a self-help book for people who want to learn from their everday experiences to improve the quality of their lives. The book will show you how to re-view, and how to use what you see to grow and develop.

The book describes a number of different ways to Wisborough, by re-viewing different types of experiences. These range from quick, simple reviews, such as "Yellow Sheets" to use routinely every day or week, to more in depth reviews, such as the "Five Step Process" to review a specific event or for personal development over a period of time.

Who can Wisborough?

Anyone can use the book as it covers experiences from work and home. Examples from work include: working more successfully with your team, managing your boss, solving problems, and using meetings more effectively. Examples from home include: improving your relationship with your partner, understanding and expressing your feelings, and helping your children discuss problems with you.

Although specific examples are shown for work and home, you will be able to adapt different review methods to suit your current situation and level of personal development. It encourages you to see your life as a whole, instead of in separate compartments.

Finding your way through the book

Each chapter stands on its own so that you can dip into the book, rather than have to start at the beginning. You can look up something which is of particular interest to you at the moment, or an issue you are trying to deal with.

However, as a general rule, we have written the book so that the chapters follow on from each other. We have tried to make sure that the easiest and least time consuming Wisboroughs are at the beginning. We have also tried to introduce concepts in the same way.

The first chapter explains the link between reviewing and personal development at home, and at work. It shows why regular Wisboroughs will become important to you, with your work, with your partner and with your family.

This is followed by a chapter explaining what may be stopping your personal development.

You will find your Gold Boxes, your treasure chests, in Chapter Three. You will discover how to use them to find yourself, in the midst of all your values, beliefs and perceptions of your world.

Each chapter then takes a particular type of Wisborough and shows how it can be used in different situations. For example, the chapter called "Contributions" shows how to use a re-view method with a team which has got stuck with a project, how we used it with three managers to look at their relationships and how to work more positively together, and finally how families can use this approach to carry out monthly reviews.

Each chapter has examples which you can quickly and easily identify with, as well as exercises to help you stop and think about different aspects of your life. You can decide what you want to change and start to do so, at your own pace.

The final chapter shows you how to let go of old beliefs and create your world for the future, so that you can be true to yourself and fulfill your life potential. Regular Wisboroughs will give you choices and a belief that change is possible.

Discovering your own solutions

This is a very practical book. It has not been written for you to simply read, but to help you feel, think and practise different ways of being yourself. We have read lots of books, in our search for self development, which have given information and concepts. We have read avidly, expecting to discover ways to deal practically with the issues raised, only to find a hundred and fifty pages of explanation and only five pages of practical ways to change. This can be very frustrating if you are ready to change your life, rather than simply read about it.

This doesn't mean that we have written a book full of ready made solutions. We do not believe in telling people what they should or should not do. The Wisborough re-view and development process will help you discover your own solutions. The book shows you different ways to find them.

We have tried to share an approach which has helped us discover ourselves and how we can live our lives more joyfully. We hope that this book will help you in the same way. We hope you enjoy the Wisborough process as well as benefit from the results. After all life is for living. It is all about the process. Our society often seems to value results more than the ways we achieve them. We hope this book will help you celebrate both.

CHAPTER ONE

DO YOU WANT TO WISBOROUGH?

Your First Wisborough

You picked up this book for a reason. Perhaps it's because you are simply curious. Or perhaps you are interested in your personal self development. Perhaps you've recently lost your job and are not sure what to do now. Perhaps you're not happy with your relationship with your partner, or your parents, or your boss. Perhaps you feel angry or sad too often. Perhaps you're very successful and don't want to lose it. Perhaps you feel ruled by "shoulds" and "oughts". Perhaps you feel trapped in a situation. Perhaps you feel you have lost your way. Perhaps you can't make a choice.

It may be none of these reasons. There are too many to list here. So, why have YOU picked it up?

By asking yourself this question, you have started to Wisborough. You have begun to think about yourself and what is important in your life at the moment. You have begun to check out what you want and why. Soon you will be trying to work out what you can change and what you can maintain.

This is the Wisborough process - "review" (re-view) and then develop. And then keep doing it. As Betty Edwards says, "A creative individual intuitively sees possibilities for transforming ordinary data into a new creation" - taken from Drawing on the Right Side of the Brain. Wisboroughs are about your own unique transformation and creation.

1

Use Wisboroughs to:

- Review and learn from everything you do, your successes as well as your mistakes

- Make connections between life experiences at home, at work and socially

- Solve work and relationships problems more easily

- Identify patterns of thoughts and feelings over time (when are you happy, angry, anxious, sad, confident?) and their effect on your relationships

- Link your thoughts and feelings to your behaviour (e.g. why are you being a martyr, being aggressive, talking so much, blaming others?)

- Explore choices, identify consequences and make decisions

- Discover a different perspective

- Safely challenge your perceptions of situations, your relation-ships and yourself

- Identify your values and beliefs and explore their effect on the way you live your life

- Plan new experiences and opportunities for learning

- Enjoy your successes

- Take care of, and be true to yourself.

As you can see, Wisboroughs can be used for personal development in the workplace, at home and socially. When working with groups in an organisation we review all aspects of life, rather than just work. Work and home affect each other. If we are angry at work it will have an effect on others at home, if we are worried at home, it will have an effect on colleagues at work, etc.

What Would You Like to Know More About?

The questionnaire below will help you think about yourself in various situations. It will help you identify issues you would like to know more about.

Rate yourself 1 - 5 against the statements below, where 1 represents never and 5 represents always. For instance, in answer to the statement "I am creative", I may see myself as never creative at home, often creative at work and generally as a reasonably creative person. I might therefore put a number 1 in the column under home, 4 in the work column and 3 in the last column.

Where we have used the word "work" in the questionnaire you may like to think of it as unpaid, rather than paid work, e.g. being a school governor, running a scout troop, being the secretary of the football team or the W.I.

There are no right and wrong answers. The aim of the questionnaire is to give you some clues about the way you see yourself and your life.

Wisboroughs

STATEMENT	AT HOME	AT WORK	ANYWHERE
I solve problems easily	4	3	3
I am creative	1	2	2
I know about myself	3	5	3
I accept change readily	3	3	2
I am a "team player"	5	3	2
I use my skills successfully	4	4	3
I work hard	5	5	5
I have fun	3 4	3	2
I am self motivated	4	4	5
I am not stressed	3	4	2
I feel healthy	3	2	4
I am in tune with myself	3	4	5
I am in tune with others	4	4	3
I am unafraid	1	2	3

Do You Want To Wisborough

STATEMENT	AT HOME	AT WORK	ANYWHERE
I am aware of my feelings	4	3	3
I express my feelings	5	3	3
I know the effect my feelings have	5	4	3
I am joyful	4	3	3
I am in control of my life	4	4	4 ~~5~~
I know where my values come from	5	3	5
I follow my spiritual beliefs	5	5	5
I am honest with myself	~~4~~ 5	3	3
I am honest with others	5	3	3
I know what I want	5	5	5
I am successful	~~3~~ 4	3	3
I fulfill my true potential	3	3	3

STATEMENT	AT HOME	AT WORK	ANYWHERE
I have successful relationships	4	3	3
I am self confident	2	3	3
I love myself as I am	2	3	3
TOTAL	109	99	96

The questionnaire shows you patterns which you can use to discover more about yourself.

Looking for clues

What do your total scores tell you? Do they tell you that you are more yourself at home, or at work, or is there little difference? What patterns do you see? It may be easier to identify them in one setting rather than another.

When you look at this list you may find that you tend to be most interested in one of the three columns. If so, you might like to look at the balance of energy and activity in your life. Sometimes we find that all of our energy is going into work and that there is nothing left for home or ourselves. If you are a woman with small children you may realise that your energy is totally put into home and that you are not giving yourself any time.

You may realise that you think your work is boring and so you put all your energy into a sport, such as cycling or jogging. This has perhaps now taken over all your time and thoughts outside work. We all need a balance. Are you happy with yours? If not, what would you like to change?

Some people find it easier to make changes at home, while others find it easier at work. So, when trying to change you may find it easier to start by concentrating on an area where you feel safe.

Do the clues show you that you behave differently in different settings? What are the differences? You are, actually, the same person wherever you are. You may like to think how true this is for you. When is it the real you and when are you acting? Do you know?

Following up the clues

Has this list helped you identify areas that you would like to work on? For instance, your problem solving, your relationship with your boss or your partner, the need to develop your skills so that you can change jobs, reduce your stress levels at work or at home, deal with conflict in your work team, discuss your concerns about your children with your partner, be less afraid, or be more confident. You can now begin to explore ways of doing this.

This questionnaire has given you a taste of Wisboroughs. If you haven't already done so, you might like to spend some time now thinking about what your answers have shown you. We hope that it has shown you how much you can discover just by stopping to think about yourself. You increase your awareness of your world by gathering information. You open up possibilities for choice and change. It is the first stage, the re-view. It is necessary to see what you want to change before you start to try to grow and develop. The second stage, development, is about planning and following this through with action. You can decide how much you want to do, when and at what pace.

Why Do a Wisborough?

During our lives we have attended many different workshops and courses. We, like everyone else, went to school for about eleven years. We learned a great deal, generally more about the theory than the practice. Some of our friends learned very little from their school lessons. Some of our friends found the learning useful to them in their lives and were able to apply it. Others never did see the point and could never apply it.

However, we also learned things that we were not taught. We learned from the playground, we learned from what made teachers cross, we learned from what was not said, as well as what was, and we learned from watching other people or thinking about things ourselves. We have discovered that the most effective way of learning about anything, including ourselves, other people and living our lives, has come from experiencing situations and reviewing regularly.

People have always reviewed when things went wrong. If the England football team is winning matches everyone cheers but when they lose everyone starts to ask what went wrong. They start to analyse the tactics, blame individual players, blame the manager or the policy of the team. We often blame other people for what has happened when we review in this way.

Sometimes we blame ourselves, and feel guilty or angry. When our lives are running smoothly, we are enjoying our work, home is calm, and the children are doing well at school, we do not stop to ask why. We just keep going, but then, when someone loses their job, a partner leaves, or the children are badly behaved, we start to ask what went wrong.

It is difficult to be analytical while we are blaming ourselves or other people, and we learn little about how to do things better next time.

Learning from everything we do

However, we can review when things go well. There is no blame of others or ourselves, there are no feelings of guilt or anger. We can pat ourselves on the back, look at our achievements, and see how hard we've worked. We feel motivated, and often inspired to continue to grow and develop.

Reviewing is about learning. We have all been told, "learn from your mistakes", but we can also learn from our successes. Indeed, we can learn from everything we do; if we review it.

The theories of learning in this way are well established. Kolb wrote about experiential learning in the 1960s. Honey & Mumford have helped people recognise how they learn and what they can do to learn more effectively. Both Kolb and Honey & Mumford base their theories on the need to review experiences.

Using Wisboroughs to improve relationships at home and at work

Not only can we learn, but we are more likely to have healthy relationships, and be whole people, valuing ourselves if we regularly review what we are doing and why.

Our relationships with ourselves, and others, are central to the quality of our lives. We enjoy results but relationships give us the opportunity to enjoy the process of working together to achieve them. This is true whether we are talking about individuals and teams within organisations, or individuals within partnerships and families. Successful relationships are those where people are involved, and are straight with one another, saying what they want, rather than worrying about upsetting or pleasing each other. In families, everyone works together towards whatever the family believes is important. In this way families even enjoy Christmas!

A healthy, honest relationship allows individuals to be whole and enjoy the process of living. It encourages each individual to achieve and discourages co-dependency. People are not dependent on their achievements or on each other for their own sense of self worth. Regular Wisboroughs help us to remember this.

The Right Time to Wisborough

If you review daily, either on your own or as part of a group, it can be done very quickly as a way to start, or finish, the day. Problems can be identified and dealt with early and speedily. You can also quickly spot issues which you are not dealing with and begin to explore your reasons for leaving them. Problems which you would not normally bother with, but which "keep eating away at you", can be cleared out so that you can start each day with a fresh perspective.

For instance, if a colleague has arrived late for the last four meetings, it may now have become so annoying to us that our behaviour at meetings is based on anger. Rather than trying to ignore it, a review early on would have prompted us to deal with the lateness, while it was still a minor irritation. We could then have mentioned it to him the first time. This is a small issue which we may not normally take up. However, we can see how this has led to us behaving negatively at meetings.

Long-term monthly and weekly reviews are also valuable as they encourage us to identify patterns which have built up over a longer period. These may not be visible from the daily reviews. We are less involved with the day to day activities by this stage and can analyse more dispassionately. It is these longer term reviews which often show us how much we have achieved, motivate us and give us the energy to do more.

For instance, you might share with your partner what you have done during the last month. You might realise that you have been avoiding a problem about one of your children or that you have avoided dealing with an issue with your childminder. You can then explore why and decide what you would like to do.

We are usually more positive about ourselves and our work when we have done a weekly or monthly Wisborough. Personal development is a slow process. The results are not always visible day to day and it is easy to become disheartened, believing that we have not moved on at all. Comparing our behaviour at the beginning and the end of the month shows us just how much we have learned. When we have recorded these reviews we have found it incredibly useful to look back at our notes for the last six months and see how much progress we have made.

Reviewing specific projects, problems or events

We can also re-view specific issues or projects. If we have a particular problem we are finding difficult because we can't see the wood for the trees, a review will help us stand back and see everything more clearly. We often try to find the solution without this clear view. This may lead us to solve the wrong problem and, to our surprise, we suddenly realise that the original problem is still there.

The review slows the problem solving process down because we are taking time to ask ourselves questions, but it is likely to give a more complete and appropriate solution, which we feel able to follow through. It is important to make sure that this type of review is thorough, ensuring that achievements as well as difficulties are identified, before looking for solutions. This ensures that all perspectives are considered and that the problem is kept in proportion. We may decide we do not have a problem at all or that it is much more manageable than we thought.

It is useful to build regular, short-term and long-term, reviews into projects, so that small problems can be dealt with before they get out of hand, and so that we do not lose sight of the overall direction. We can also see at an early stage if we are unlikely to be able to achieve our objectives. We can then replan as necessary.

Wisboroughs With Your Team

We learn a lot from specific events if we review them at the time, e.g if your management team have just given a presentation to the workforce it could be useful for your team to review what exactly happened, what seemed to go well, what seemed less successful and to check each person's perception of the event and its outcomes. From this, your team can think about how they would do it differently next time and so learn from their experience.

Regular reviews with your work group or team help you look both at the outcomes and the process. By this we mean that the group can review what they have achieved and not achieved, as well as how they worked together to do this.

Using reviews to work with teams evolved from our work as management trainers. Chrissie's work as a relationships counsellor had led us to give teams the opportunity to explore difficult events in a safe setting. Within this safe setting it was possible to review relationships within teams and see their effect upon the work of the teams. We could then help teams find ways to improve the way they worked together to be more successful.

Our reviews helped teams explore different aspects of their relationships. Competition and conflict between group members could be explored by looking at what people had said and done, both in previous situations and during the review group meeting. Having identified the conflicts, we were able to use them positively. Teams became less afraid of conflict and could see that it was actually valuable. They found that the energy from conflict could lead to greater creativity if it was appropriately channelled. This is always a great breakthrough for teams which have previously felt unable to work together constructively.

We were often told that a conflict could never be resolved because it was simply a "personality clash". Reviewing values showed team members that they had conflicting <u>values</u>, rather than conflicting <u>personalities</u>. The total team value is made up of individual member's values, even if they are different, e.g. the sales manager and the production manager. Therefore, team members can learn to acknowledge and respect each others values as they contribute to the total team value. Value differences are often mistaken for personality clashes.

As team members are individuals with different experiences and backgrounds, they have different perspectives. These different perspectives can be very useful to a group as individuals will see the problem from different angles and offer a number of different solutions. It can also help the team understand more about the way they work together as everyone will see this differently too. But different perspectives are only useful to a team if they are heard and valued. The review process encourages this to happen.

Some groups we worked with did not display open conflict, but had an air of cosyness. In fact, members colluded to avoid anything which might have been upsetting, so that they all just did what they knew they were all happy to do. By reviewing their behaviour it was possible to see that many issues had been avoided and that the team was stagnating, rather than developing as a team, or developing fresh ideas. This could also be seen by the way people spoke to each other and behaved towards each other. By reviewing its behaviour (words and actions) a team can learn to deal with issues more assertively and so work more creatively together.

Team roles

Wisboroughs with groups always highlight the different roles which individuals take. It also shows the degree of polarisation within each team. This often contributes towards teams and families repeating the same patterns of behaviour and makes it difficult for them to work in a different way. Individuals who want to change their behaviour find it difficult as others are used to the specific roles and the particular polarizing which has become the norm for the group.

Regular Wisboroughs help individuals maintain new behaviour and help the team manage its feelings about the changed behaviour within the group.

Once a team begins to recognise the polarisation taking place, people begin to recognise the way in which they each contribute to any issue or problem the team has. Teams tend to believe that a problem is usually owned by an individual, e.g. in a team we worked with, Jonathan was seen as the aggressive one and Margaret was seen as "a walkover". During a review this polarisation was identified.

Jonathan and Margaret were able to say that although they were comfortable in these roles, they also admitted that they didn't like always having to take them.

The team were then able to look at how the roles were given by everyone and how Jonathan and Margaret were willing to take them on. The rest of the team were also able to explore why they avoided taking these roles and were so happy to give them to Jonathan and Margaret.

Finally, the team were able to work out how to help each other polarise less, and help each other be more assertive.

Instead of these problems remaining as Jonathan and Margaret's, the whole team took them on as a team problem, ownership was shared. They all contributed to the solution and had a stake in making sure that it worked.

The success of a team is dependent upon everyones contribution to it. Problems are often given to individuals but can best be solved by the whole team. Reviewing by the team helps them own the problems they identify, even if one person is asked to carry out specific actions.

The team v. the rest

We have used Wisboroughs to help teams look at their relationships with other departments in their organisation. This is a similar process to that of helping individuals review their relationships within a team. In one organisation, we reviewed the relationship between three departments, marketing, sales and after-sales service, which had to work together. Having examined the way that the three departments behaved towards each other, and explored their feelings about each other they realised that they all had different value bases. They all thought different things were important.

They were then able to work out what their relationships could be. They discovered that they shared some common values and could see the importance of the differences as these actually enabled the organisation to meet its objectives. The teams redefined the workloads of each department in the light of this new knowledge.

Your team can use the review process to identify its position within the organisation. You can discover how you are seen by different parts of the organisation and why you are treated in a particular way, e.g. as the superior salesmen, or the stuffy accountants or the pompous personnel department, etc. You can choose what identity you would like and how to work towards achieving it. As one team said "I want to be a tomato!".

If teams within your organisation Wisborough regularly the whole culture of the organisation can change. People understand more about their own values and the organisation's values.

They use their day to day work to learn from, take responsibility for team and organisational issues, and ultimately for the success or failure of the company.

Just as teams and departments can review and change their position in an organisation, so too can the whole organisation do the same with its position with other organisations and even the rest of the world.

A Wisborough With Your Partner

Having seen how the review and development process worked for individuals and teams within organisations, we realised that we could use Wisboroughs in our own relationship. We had both been in previous relationships where issues had been avoided. No aspects of these relationships had ever really been discussed, never mind reviewed. We did not want our relationship to follow the same path. It is very easy for people, after a divorce, to remarry and fall into exactly the same traps again. We wanted our relationship this time to be better, as we knew that ultimately the pain of avoiding issues was much greater than the pain of facing uncomfortable facts.

As in organisations, couples often review when things go wrong. Usually, this leads to an argument, blame is laid, blame is denied, guilt is thrown and felt, but nothing is analysed or resolved. Often issues are quietly locked away, only to appear again at another time, perhaps in a different guise but still needing attention. Reviewing regularly means that good times are reviewed as well as bad times, learning takes place and the relationship develops.

We discovered regular reviewing for our own relationship after we had been living together for about a year. We thought we had a good relationship but when we started reviewing regularly we realised that it was getting better. Tiny incidents were dealt with very quickly, as they had not been forgotten and allowed to grow. We each understood how the other had seen a specific incident. We didn't have to try to guess what the other might be feeling or worry about it. We used the Wisborough to discuss our feelings.

We realised that no harm came to us by discussing issues that earlier we had avoided, or ignored, or tried to forget. Previously we had often not raised issues because we had been afraid that they might upset the other person or lead to an argument. Wisboroughs taught us to be more courageous, and over time, we realised that it took less courage as we were less afraid. The reviews also encouraged us to be much more open and honest with each other. Our relationship developed as the trust between us grew. This lead us to be more honest with ourselves and less afraid of discovering our own feelings, especially if previously we believed such feelings to be negative or bad. Wisboroughs worked for us.

Initially we re-viewed daily so that small things were picked up early and so that we enjoyed the good times more. We became much more aware of the positive happenings. We felt more positive about our relationship and ourselves.

We discovered from doing a monthly Wisborough as well, that we learned even more. We were able to spot patterns of behaviour, thoughts and feelings which were affecting our relationship. It was particularly helpful to spot the traps. We saw when we were polarising, as in our past relationships. We looked at the reasons for this and worked out what we could do to stop it.

For instance, we discovered that whenever Chrissie felt she was "for ever tidying the house", it was because she had decided to take on the responsiblity for keeping the house tidy, while Richard had given up any responsibility in that area. Having realised this, we explored why we had both slipped back into this pattern of responsibilities. We talked about our feelings and worked out how we wanted to do it differently. This stopped Chrissie simply being fed up or nagging and stopped Richard feeling vaguely guilty and running around trying to please.

You can see from this example how Wisboroughs will give you a much greater understanding of what is happening in your relationship, a greater understanding of the difficulties you have, an opportunity to change and a greater awareness of your own hopes and fears. Your relationship will be much stronger and more honest as a result of regular Wisboroughs.

You Can Do Wisboroughs With Your Children

We found that it was possible to include Chrissie's son, Philip, in the review process so that as a family we could have more understanding of the effect we all had on each other. Families often only review at times of crisis, e.g when a child starts to truant, when a parent is made redundant, when someone becomes ill, when parents want to divorce or one partner is found to be having an affair. When everything is running smoothly we do not ask ourselves why. We only ask why when things start to go wrong. As we have already seen, there is then too much blame, guilt or anger to be able to gain very much from the situation.

Philip learned to express his feelings about incidents. He has become more aware of his own feelings, and when he is blocking more of his view of the world and what is happening between us all.

He often understood what was happening, not only between us, but also between himself and his father, and himself and his own friends. Philip knows the effect his behaviour has on others and can see patterns of behaviour building up over time. He is able to identify when someone else's behaviour is intended to make him feel guilty, or when someone is aggressive because they are frightened.

Wisboroughs can help you improve your interpersonal skills. You can learn to listen more attentively to each other, check out the real meaning of statements, ask questions and be unambiguous.

Philip has been able to take these skills into other situations so that he can benefit in these too. For instance, he was able to ask a teacher at school why he had been reprimanded with two other boys when he didn't think that he deserved it. As he asked assertively, the teacher did not think he was being cheeky or aggressive, but that he believed he had the right to ask and to expect an answer. The teacher was then able to answer him honestly without feeling defensive.

You can see how our family has benefited from Wisboroughs. So can yours.

Keeping Notes of Your Learning

As you can see from all our examples, personal development can take place in all situations. You will find it useful to keep some notes of your reviews as personal development can sometimes leave you feeling that you have made a great effort for very little change or reward. When looking back over the notes for six months you will see how much progress you have made. This will inspire you to continue.

As personal development can be a lonely process, it is a good idea to share your reviews with someone else. This will give you a different perspective and you will feel supported. Writing notes or talking to someone collects and clarifies your thoughts. This way you see things you had not seen before. If you write notes your internal "little self" will know that you intend to take action. Writing notes and sharing them with someone is a very powerful way of convincing yourself that you are serious about making changes.

Making a Start

We have found that many people spend time reading about self development, know lots of different theories, but continually avoid putting them into practise. You may recognise yourself here. The next chapter will help you discover what is stopping you. Feeling reluctant is a very healthy self protection device. We don't need to chastise ourselves for this or for what we think or feel. We can simply ask ourselves why, so that we can learn from our thoughts and feelings.

You can use the next chapter to explore your reluctance and dispel any fears about personal development.

We hope that you will read on and learn to enjoy life more.

CHAPTER TWO

WHAT STOPS US?

What Stops You Changing?

What stops you re-viewing and developing? What stops you:

- hearing the messages you are receiving from other people?

- looking at your own behaviour?

- looking at the patterns that you keep repeating?

- looking for meaning?

- asking yourself questions?

- challenging yourself?

- knowing what you want?

- asking for what you want?

- changing?

- wanting to change?

What might stop you doing the Wisboroughs in this book?

Time

Well, the first thing you might say is that you don't have time. Is this really true? You might like to think about what you've done during the last few days. Have you done things that:

- you didn't need to,

- other people could have done,

- you could have spent less time on,

- you didn't really enjoy,

- you thought were a waste of time?

You can use a review and development process for as little as ten minutes a day. If you stopped to answer these questions you have already started to Wisborough.

Another reason for not reviewing regularly is that we often believe that it is selfish to take time out for ourselves. Personal reflection may be considered too self-centred. If you are used to spending your time taking care of, or being responsible for others you may find it difficult to stop worrying about them and to take care of yourself. You may not think you are important enough.

Have you thought about who suffers when you are not looking after yourself and who benefits when you feel good about yourself? Imagine how much better everyone will be when you not only feel good about yourself, but are also more knowledgable and skillful.

What have you done in the last few days that was as important to you as your own care and development?

Learning is an academic exercise

Until recently everyone at school learned in a passive way. "I teach, you learn." This does not encourage us to have confidence in the belief that we can teach ourselves. So, you may be inclined to want to read this book and treat it as an academic exercise rather than a practical one.

For many of us, reading is a solitary experience that goes on in our heads. It is not an experience we share with others or use to learn about ourselves in our everyday lives. Often the only books which prompt us to take action are instruction manuals or recipe books. You may find it useful to think of this book in that way. As any cook will tell you, the best recipes are those you take and adapt for yourself. Wisboroughs are for adapting.

Self development even takes place when we read novels for pleasure. You may believe that you can only learn from text books. But, when you read a novel you identify with the characters and think about the way your life is reflected by the book.

Lack of confidence

Perhaps you don't think you can change, or try out new behaviours or think about life differently. Perhaps you expect the exercises in the book to be too difficult. You may not feel confident enough.

Life experiences may have left you lacking the confidence to try to change your life, or learn something new. Perhaps you have been in the same job for a long time, or have been looking after small children, or have been out of work, or were not clever at school or have no qualifications. You've been brave enough to open this book. It's a first step.

When we lack confidence we can only begin to make the changes if we take small steps and practise in safe situations. We have tried to emphasise the importance of this throughout the book. Only you can know what you feel able to do. Better to have small successes than a big failure which will damage your confidence even more. Use the book to help you take these small steps in your own time. Only take risks when you feel ready to.

Keeping our image of ourselves

You might think, as one chief executive with a large car and a smart suit said, "all this sort of thing doesn't concern me". It didn't fit his image of himself. We all have a self image. It includes how we think we should look and how we think we should behave. For some of us it is difficult to admit that we might need to develop. We think we are supposed to already know the answers. We believe we shouldn't need any help. Perhaps we have always dismissed ideas about self help and believe we can't be seen to change now.

We may have taken up positions to maintain our self image and fear moving from them. The problem is that the image takes the place of our real self and we begin to fear our real self being discovered. We spend a lot of time and energy maintaining the image and hiding our real selves. We could use this energy to discover and develop.

This fear of being found out or of discovering ourselves to be bad, is often (a hidden) reason why we don't review. We have found that the review process, generally, shows us that we are not as bad as we feared. People often find that they are more lovable than they thought. It is only possible to come to this knowledge by discovering your true self and acknowledging all your different parts. By identifying the bits which you don't like about yourself as well as those you do, you can begin to accept them all as legitimate parts of yourself. If you want to change them, you can then consciously choose to do so.

Sometimes we have feelings which we think are bad and which we do not want to look at or even admit to. We think that if we have these feelings <u>we</u> must be bad. We learn this belief as children.

For instance, Richard believed that it was bad to be angry and so he rarely was. However, he has since discovered that having anger is as much a part of him as any other emotion. As a human being he was given anger as a positive force to protect himself and to bring about change. What he has had to learn is not that anger is bad, but how to express it and use it appropriately.

There are, in fact, no parts of us which are bad. They all just are. We are whole people but may get used to only using particular parts to play particular characters in particular scenes.

We tend to think that we are imperfect and thefore look for the imperfections in others rather than look for their lovableness. If we can find <u>their</u> imperfections we hope that it will show us that we aren't so bad after all. Someone said "God does not make rubbish". We are all perfect as we are. You may like to think how this idea could affect your view of yourself and others. If we can accept ourselves as we are we can begin to accept other people as they are too.

Wanting to be liked

Our fear of being discovered goes hand in hand with our fear of not being liked. While reviewing, we may discover a behaviour or an attitude which we would like to change. We may stop reviewing if we believe that changing will make someone dislike us. We decide not to put into practise what we have learned.

For instance, John always stayed late at work to finish things off because his boss never managed to give them to him until the end of the day. He wanted to change this and say "no" sometimes but found that he couldn't do this. He believed that his boss would not like him if he did. He even believed that he would be fired because he would no longer be doing what his boss wanted. He knew that the requests were unreasonable.

At home you may find yourself agreeing to go and see a film with your partner when you want to go to a concert. You do not say what you would really like to do because you want your partner to like you and you believe he will be displeased with you if you say what you really want.

We worked with someone once who had learned the "right behaviour". Brian knew how to behave assertively, angrily, and with sadness but this was completely divorced from his feelings. He was acting; behaving in the "correct" way. Behaving in this learned way did not help him feel good. As Brian had to act most of the time, he was never quite sure of his real feelings and those around him were never sure either. Brian believed he had to be seen as a "nice guy" in order to be liked. He was concerned that if he looked at what he was really like, he might discover that he was not nice and therefore could not be liked.

Reviewing usually helps with these fears because we begin to see that they are unfounded. Firstly, we may discover that generally people like us. Secondly, by reviewing our changes in behaviour regularly, we can monitor the effect they are having on other people. We will probably find that we are more respected than previously. Finally, we will begin to like and respect ourselves more.

Fear of failure

Often we don't start anything new because we fear failure. We talk about things as good ideas for a very long time. We do nothing about them in case we do not successfully achieve them. We believe that it's better to think what might have been, than to risk putting our plans into action. We forget that we can enjoy the process of doing, as much as that of achieving.

Part of any Wisborough is planning how to tackle new things. We can build in steps small enough to ensure success. We are more likely to succeed if we review regularly, take small steps and have small successes to encourage us. We can always alter our course of action if we find that we are losing our way, or losing heart.

I don't need therapy

Many people view personal development programmes as therapy for people with serious problems. If this is your view you may be reluctant to use this book as you know that you don't have a serious problems.

As we said earlier, we originally used the review and development process as a training and management technique. Only later did we start to use it for ourselves, not because we thought we needed therapy, but because we thought we could use it to improve our already successful relationship and business partnership. We have since discovered that Wisboroughs can be used at a number of different levels. They can be used to deal with the minor issues of everyday life as well as the major crises. We use them to learn as much as we can from our everyday experiences.

The Hidden Blocks to Change

Not opening the Gold Boxes

The black box in an aeroplane is used to discover why the aeroplane has crashed. It contains useful information which can be used to prevent other crashes. Similarly, we can think of the messages in our unconscious as information in a gold box.

We can think of our gold boxes as treasure chests; full of useful information. We often do not open our gold boxes until after we have crashed. There has to be a major disaster in our lives, such as an illness, the death of a close friend, a partner leaving, or losing a job, before we will look at the information we have stored about our lives.

Just as the information in the black box of an aeroplane has to be interpreted, so the information in our own gold boxes has to be interpreted. What we hope to do with the review and development process is to review the information and interpret it before a crash.

Ignoring the signals

We may have signals from our body, other people and our life situations, that all is not well. We may be overstretched, either financially or in time or energy. We may feel stressed, or become ill. People may avoid us, or we may avoid situations. We may find ourselves in too many situations which make us angry, or frightened. We can use these signals as prompts to review the contents of our gold boxes, rather than wait until the crash. We often ignore the signals, and may even try to cover them up. We do not want to see or acknowledge that there is anything wrong.

For instance, if my partner is habitually coming home from work late, I may not want to think that he is unhappy in our relationship. So, I will believe him when he says that he has to work so hard to earn enough to maintain our current lifestyle. I will tell everyone how hard he works. I will be really grateful if he comes home on time with a bunch of flowers. He must love me, mustn't he? I will do all of this, rather than discuss and explore with him the causes. So I will not discover the information we need to decide what we can do to change things.

Feeling too confused

One of the reasons we do not like working with the information from our unconscious, is that we can easily feel confused and overwhelmed by it.

We think of the gold box containing another which contains other gold boxes. It is rather like a set of Russian Dolls which fit inside each other. We can choose which box to work with. We have found the concept of the gold boxes useful to give a structure to interpret the information contained in our unconscious. The gold boxes help us reduce our confusion. They help us begin to see some of our own personal patterns of thoughts, feelings and behaviour. We can use these to look at what we feel able to work with at the moment.

Changing more than your behaviour

You may have found that you want to change your behaviour in a particular situation. You work very hard to bring about the change and may even feel that it is happening for a while, but quickly find that you fall back into old behaviours. You become disillusioned, give up and feel even worse about yourself.

Anna wanted to lose weight. She would diet and lose some weight but couldn't stick to a diet. She may have found it useful to look at why she ate too much, or why she was always overweight, or why she didn't really want to be slimmer or why she thought she should be slimmer.

The set of gold boxes idea can help you, as it not only lets you see patterns of behaviour, but also helps you to see some of the underlying reasons for them. These underlying causes may need to be tackled if there is to be a long term change in your behaviour.

Our behaviour is only the outward sign of what is going on inside us. I may behave differently if:

- I feel calmer, or

- I like myself more, or

- I am no longer afraid of being "discovered", or

-   I am doing what I want to do rather than trying to please others, etc.

When I say I want to change, what I tend to mean is that I want to change the unseen parts of me so that I feel better, as well as change my behaviour. However, the only way <u>you</u> will notice that I have changed is because I behave differently or say different things.

You may like to use your gold boxes to discover what is stopping you reviewing or changing. The next chapter describes how you can look at what your gold boxes contain.

CHAPTER THREE

MAKING GOLD BOXES WORK FOR YOU

The Set of Gold Boxes

You can use Gold Boxes to sort out the confusion you may feel when you start to look at your life.

You will see from the diagram below that your Gold Boxes consist of:

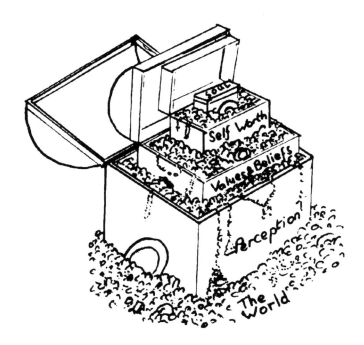

- your World

- your Perception

- your Values and Beliefs

- your Self-Worth

- your Soul

Gold Boxes will help you explore your world, check your perceptions, see the effect of your values and beliefs, realise your self-worth and discover your soul.

This is another way of thinking of the Gold Boxes

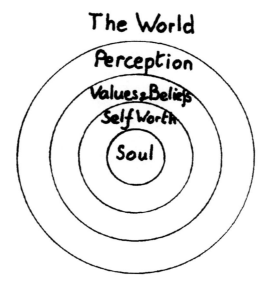

"The World"

"The World" outside the gold boxes is the one with which we are all most familiar. It includes all the information we have about our lives, including our behaviour and the behaviour of those around us.

We often do not see what is going on around us or notice things. To become more aware of "the World", you may find it useful to write descriptions of events or situations, including what people have said and done. This slows your world down so that you can consciously see it.

"The World" is the area with which we are most familiar but it is the area in which many people get stuck. Changes in this are seen as an end in themselves because this is seen as the "real world". People usually go on courses to learn how to change the way they do things. They learn new skills. We do not believe that this, in itself, is always enough.

Back-sliding

Peter was on an assertiveness course that we ran. He learned assertive behaviour very quickly and went and tried it out. He was delighted to find that it "worked". However, a month after the course he was unable to maintain the behaviour because he had not looked at why he did not normally behave assertively. He said he thought such "navel gazing unnecessary".

It is very difficult to maintain learned behaviour in any setting, (at work or at home), if it is not a true reflection of our inner selves. We often confuse other people because it is difficult to completely cover up our underlying true selves. Our true selves leak out different messages from the words we are saying; our body language says different things from our words. Added to this we have the hidden fear of being discovered. We try to hide our inner selves even more. We begin to lose touch with ourselves and, far from the change in behaviour making us happy, it causes us further stress.

We are not saying here that only learning to change your behaviour is wrong. Sometimes practising new behaviour successfully will make you feel more confident and then more able to explore your attitudes and so maintain the new behaviour. In "Self Healing: Use Your Mind to Heal Your Body", Louis Proto says "If you can't make it, fake it" until you can. You can use the change in behaviour as a start to making a whole change; in both your inner and outer self. Using learned behaviour will be more successful and you will feel better about yourself if it is part of a holistic approach to personal development.

Examining our world gives us useful information. We now need to look at how we interpret it.

"Perception"

The first gold box, "Perception" contains our interpretations of "The World". When we look at our interpretations we begin to realise that our description of events is often different from other peoples. We all have our own view of reality. We all live on this earth and all believe that we live in the same world. In fact, we all live in our own worlds. We see different things, and place a different emphasis on the importance of actions and events.

You might like to ask a friend to write a description of the view from a window, while you do the same. Then exchange your descriptions and look at the similarities and differences.

If we add our thoughts and feelings to our descriptions of the world we can see the effect they have. Our thoughts and feelings affect our behaviour, which in turn affects other people. We can use our descriptions to see this effect.

Our interpretation of situations will depend upon how we collect information from the world. For instance, some of us tend to look for positive aspects in situations, while others tend to look for negative ones. So, two different people can pick up different information from the same event.

Self-fulfilling prophesies

Our thoughts affect what information we pick up, how we interpret it, and how we behave in response to it. So, if I think someone doesn't like me I expect her to put me down and I do not hear the compliments she pays me. I may behave aggressively towards her as I am expecting her to be horrid to me. Then, when she is horrid, in response to me, I pick up this information and store it. I have made myself a self fulfilling prophesy. We can interrupt this thought process by changing our perception (as we show in Chapter Ten).

To help people use the contents of this Gold Box we ask them to challenge their perceptions by writing questions to help each other explore their descriptions of "The World" and their "Perception". They examine the conclusions they have drawn from their interpretations of "The World". People start thinking about change, by observing behaviour and consciously collecting different data.

For instance, I think I make poor presentations. So, when I go to meetings, I always look for Sue's frowns to confirm that I do. I can challenge my perception. I can check out the data that has lead me to this conclusion. In future meetings I will look to see what everyone in the group does when I speak. I may find that they are smiling! This will affect my view of my reality.

I can also see how my feelings are affected by someone else's behaviour towards me and how my feelings affect my behaviour towards them. So, when Sue frowns I feel anxious. I answer her questions aggressively. She frowns some more. I feel threatened and again answer her question in a negative tone. This sets the pattern for the rest of the meeting. I am unaware that because Ann smiles I answer her questions enthusiastically. So what we are saying is "the World" affects our "Perception" and our "Perception" affects what we see as "the World".

Values and Beliefs

Our "Perception" is also influenced by the next Gold Box, "Values and Beliefs" and this affects what we see as "the World". Our values and beliefs are learned early; from our parents, teachers, and friends at school. We reinforce these throughout our lives. Sometimes we change them, but it is difficult. It feels easier, and less confusing, if we make sure that we only see the things which maintain our original values and beliefs. So, we only see and work within a particular mind set, a particular view of the world. This stops us re-viewing with an open mind and so stops us changing.

When we talk about "values and beliefs", we mean the constructs and prejudices we carry in our heads to make sense of the world. We feel safe if we can classify things. If we believe that men don't cry, must be brave, are cleverer than women, must go to work, etc. this will affect our view of the men around us. Our beliefs about men will lead us to only see certain aspects of the men we know. We will then go on to make specific judgements about them based on those beliefs. If a man measures up to our beliefs about men, we will think that he is a good chap and like him. If he doesn't, we shall judge against him.

We only rarely question our judgements about people, or change our initial opinions about them. We even more rarely ask what values and beliefs we are using to make our judgements, where they come from, or if they are still appropriate.

What are your values and beliefs?

We have values and beliefs for all aspects of our world. We have beliefs about men and women, race, class, and religion, etc. You may find it useful to finish the following statements and add some of your own to help you identify your own values and beliefs.

Men are ...	Women are ...
Men should ...	Women should ...
Men shouldn't ...	Women shouldn't ...
Men do ...	Women do ...
Men don't ...	Women don't ...
Men ...	Women ...
Nice men ...	Nice women ...

Wisboroughs

Bad men ...   Bad women ...

Working class people are ...   Middle class people are ...

Working class people can ...   Middle class people can ...

Working class people think ... Middle class people think ...

Working class people like ...   Middle class people like ...

Working class people
                can't ...   Middle class people can't ...

Working class people ...   Middle class people ...

Black people are ...   White people are ...

Jews are ...   Greeks are ...

Americans are ...   Welsh/Scots/Irish/English are ..

People who go to church
                are ...   Evangelists are ...

You have probably now begun to think of others of your own.
Add these to your list.

You may now like to think

- where your different values and beliefs have come from (e.g.
my mother always said that ..., my grandfather was a coalminer
and a strong union man who thought ..., etc.)?

- what evidence do you now have and where do you get it from to maintain your values and beliefs (e.g. what newspapers do you choose to read, to which groups do you belong, etc.)?

Which of the statements do you think of as values and beliefs and which do you think of as prejudices? What do you see as the difference?

These are probably the most obvious values and beliefs we have, but we also have many others, often personal to ourselves to which we may be less aware. These include views about age, ("you can't teach an old dog new tricks"), and children, ("children should be seen and not heard"). You would be surprised how many people believe children should not be listened to, even though they don't admit this to themselves. We often classify people according to the jobs that they or their partners do, e.g. "he is an accountant so he must like ...", "she's a housewife so she ...", he is a policeman so ...", "she's a vicar's wife so ...", "his wife runs her own business so ...".

Family beliefs

Our own family experiences affect our beliefs about how families are or should be. We are often surprised when we realise that other families do things differently. Some questions you might like to ask yourself to clarify some of your beliefs about family life are:

What are you supposed to be like as a Mum or Dad?

What would make the perfect family?

How late should teenagers stay out?

Should children have pocket money?

Can a step parent be as good as the original parent?

When should children be taken into care?

How often should couples have sex?

Should you have sex before marriage?

What and when should children be told about sex?

What do you think of divorced women?

What do you think of divorced men?

Under what circumstances would you get divorced?

Should everyone have specific jobs to do in the house? What should they be?

Again, You can probably add lots more of your own, and again the next question is:

- why do you believe this?

- how does it affect what you do?

For instance, you may say that couples should have sex when they like, but do you feel guilty if you don't make love once a week, twice a week, once a month, etc? This is just one example of how our beliefs affect us without us realising it.

Work values

Similarly, at work we will have some values and beliefs which are our own, some which belong to the organisation we are working in now and some which come with us from previous organisations, including school. You may have noticed that communication is difficult with people from other organisations when they have different values and beliefs from your own.

You might find it useful to work out some questions with work colleagues to check out your organisation's values and beliefs. Here are some examples to start you off:

How are foremen viewed, e.g. a total waste of time, the most important people in the company?

What do you think of graduates as managers?

How useful is the research and development department?

Does your team need a leader?

Should the boss know the answers?

You can use your questions to explore

- how teams work,

- the roles of people in the organisation,

- how money and status is used within the organisation,

- how your personal or team values vary from those of the organisation,

- if your organisation's stated values match the actual day to day activities within the organisation, etc.

So, What's Stopping You?

As you can see, we use the "Values and Beliefs" Gold Box to help people challenge their values and beliefs, explore the effect they have on their "Perceptions" and their behaviour in "The World". The questions we ask a group here will be determined by the situation we are reviewing with them. When thinking about the questions and statements above you have been reviewing your own beliefs and values. You may have begun to realise that some of them are no longer appropriate for you now, they may actually be blocking your personal development.

You may have realised that your values and beliefs are fundamental to you and may be difficult to change unless you are ready. However, now you are more aware of them you can choose to modify them if you wish to.

If you go back to the previous chapter, you will see how closely your values and beliefs are linked to the things which stop you reviewing and developing, e.g. if you are an executive you may believe that you don't have time to review. This may be linked to your belief that executives should be too busy and important to have time. If you are a housewife who thinks that it would be selfish to take time to review it may be because you believe that mothers should look after the family rather than have time for themselves.

From the questions you have been asking about your values and beliefs you can probably see how much your values and beliefs can get in the way when you re-view. They not only limit your actual vision of the world, but form a barrier when you relate to other people. Looking back over the work you have just done, you might like to ask yourself

- how you use your values and beliefs to judge others?

- which ones you would now like to let go?

"Self Worth"

The next Gold Box, "Self Worth", is closely related to our "Values and Beliefs". It is used to explore the value we put on ourselves as a direct result of the general beliefs and values we hold. If I believe that a housewife should put her family before herself, I will do this in order to believe that I am a good person, i.e. have self worth. Much of this self value is tied up with our own image of ourselves, how we think we should be, look, act, etc. We use the "shoulds" and "oughts" of our "Values and Beliefs" box to reinforce and maintain our view of ourselves. This continual reinforcement prevents us changing our view of ourselves. It also prevents us changing our behaviour in "The World".

If you find youself saying you "should" do something or you "ought" to do something, you may find it interesting to ask yourself why. Your reason is probably linked to one of the values and beliefs you identified in your previous lists. Try changing the word "should" or "ought" to the word "want". How does this sound? What difference does it make to the way you feel? What are the new consequences of your actions?

I want to be good

Having tried to replace "should" and "ought" with "want", you may have discovered that the statement no longer rings true. It isn't what you want. This might mean that you value the "shoulds" and "oughts" more highly than your your own wants.

For example, I may believe that I should go and see my mother for Sunday lunch. When I replace "should" with "want" I realise that I do not want to go to Sunday lunch. I might therefore, think that I am a bad son and therefore a bad person because I don't want to do what I believe a good son should do.

What I have done is take my belief about how families should operate in our society, ("Values and Beliefs"), translate that into how I should behave as a member of a family,(how I should behave in "The World"), and then translate that further into my belief about my self ("Self-Worth"). I then used that to choose behaviour to confirm my view of myself and probably that of others too.

In this example the values are used to confirm my view of myself and my mother. I do not try a different behaviour, e.g. not go to Sunday lunch this week, go to tea instead on Tuesday, or ask my mother to come to me for lunch. It probably doesn't even occur to me that I could. I am either <u>good,</u> and go to lunch or <u>bad,</u> and don't go to lunch. I have forgotten the real reason for going to lunch - to see my mother. I am locked into what I believe is the expected behaviour if I am to see myself as a good son.

If you change your behaviour you may feel you are behaving out of character and may fear the consequences. You might be surprised if you try a change in this way, particularly if you offer the other person some other alternatives. Perhaps my mother would be relieved not to have to cook lunch for me, perhaps she would prefer to come to me occasionally, perhaps she would

like to see me during the week sometimes instead. Perhaps she
does expect me to come to lunch. At least we could discuss
what we both want, rather than just doing what we think we
should.

I want to be bad

From this, you may think that we all adopt behaviour to confirm
that we are good people. In fact, some people adopt behaviour
to confirm that they are bad people. It is still using behaviour
to translate general values and beliefs into self worth. If, as a
male manager, I believe that men are bad and should be
aggressive, then I will "bully" people at work. This behaviour
reinforces my view that I am bad which is what men should be.
I will find it difficult to change and take a more gentle approach
(no matter how many management courses I attend!) because
it will not fit my general beliefs about men or my view of myself
as a man.

Another reason I will find it difficult to change is that I believe
others will see me as weak. I do not actually know if other
people share my beliefs about men, but I am afraid to check this
out. Again, my fear of the consequences gets in the way.

Judging yourself

If you go back to the answers you gave when looking at your
"Values and Beliefs" you will find that these are the criteria you
generally use to measure your perception of your own self
worth. You use these to unconsciously make judgements about
yourself. If you would like to discover more about these
judgements take each of your statements and score yourself 0
- 10 against it - giving yourself 10 if you really match it and 0

if you don't. You have now used your criteria consciously to judge yourself.

Having done this, you may like to ask yourself;

Is this how you see yourself?

Is this how you think other people see you?

Is this how you would like to be?

Is this how you would like to be seen?

If, having done this, you tend to see yourself as either good or bad, (or want to see yourself as good for fear that you are actually bad), you may find it useful to remember that you are neither. Sometimes you <u>behave</u> badly and sometimes you <u>behave</u> well. However, your beliefs about yourself will affect how much value you put on yourself.

Continuum of self worth

Most people use external criteria to measure their own self worth. This leads to the conclusion that they are unworthy and therefore unloveable. You may find it useful to ask yourself whether you think you

- have worth and are loveable, or

- have no worth and are unloveable, or

- sometimes have worth and therefore sometimes are lovable.

If you use the external criteria (your values and beliefs listed earlier) to judge your worth and therefore your lovableness, you may find it hard to believe that you are loveable.

If you think of loveableness as being on a continuum then you can see that most people seem to work from the belief that sometimes they are loveable, but often they are not. Instead, they could work from the belief that they are generally loveable just for being themselves, whatever the external criteria.

Continuum of self worth

Worthy   Worthless

I love myself   I love some parts of   I don't love myself
                   myself sometimes

I am Loveable   I am Unloveable

If you work from the belief that you are unloveable you are likely to:

- want to please people to gain or keep love,

- fear discovery of your true self,

- behave aggressively or passively to keep people away so that your true self cannot be seen.

This uses energy and blocks growth and development. If you believe you are loveable you can look at yourself and let others see you without fear.

"Soul"

As John Bradshaw says in his book, "Creating Love The Next Great Stage of Growth":

"Soul is what is most profoundly human in each of us, and nothing human is foreign to the soul, including mistakes, failures and our pathology.

Soulfulness is not fully definable because it is a state of being. It is the state of being fully human. Being human involves body and mind, matter and spirit. Thomas Moore, in his fine book "Care of the Soul", writes: "Soul is the "in-between" factor keeping mind in touch with body and matter in touch with spirit."

We can get hints and glimmers of soul as we learn more and more about being human."

As people tend to use external criteria to judge their value, they often confuse "Self Worth" with "Soul". Andrea judges her-self by whether she sees herself as a "good" mother, a "good" wife, a "good" manager, etc. She fears that she may be worthless, so she spends a lot of time and energy trying to convince herself that she is worthy. She believes she must use the external criteria to measure her worthiness. She uses her behaviour in "The World" to judge herself. She does not look at "herself" and therefore discover her true worth.

So long as she has the energy to keep trying to meet the external criteria she finds it hard to change. She gets the rewards of feeling less negative about herself. Today she managed to behave in the "right" way most of the time and so could tell herself that she was good. She will probably only feel the need to change when she runs out of energy or when the stress catches up with her.

Unfortunately, Andrea feels a void. She talks about her fear of a black hole inside herself. She is out of touch with her "Soul". She's unwilling to make contact with this bit of herself, her core, which is always loveable and always worthy as she fears that it may not be. Instead she only defines herself by her behaviour, her values and beliefs, and her view of her "Self Worth". She believes this final "Self Worth" to be her core. She uses the information from the other boxes to describe herself. She would be unlikely to say that she is either unique or loveable. She is, of course, both.

We know this because when Andrea is completely absorbed in what she is doing, working well to the best of her ability, she forgets and is herself. It is then that her loveableness shines through. She is no longer keeping the boxes closed to form barriers to protect her core, her "Soul", and prevent it from being seen. The boxes are open, she can be seen and she can see the rest of the world. When they are closed, as we have seen, they work as filters so that she reinforces her old view of the world and herself.

You have probably recognised this feeling of being in touch with your "Soul" when you have been aware of how blue the sky is, how warm the sun is, how well you are working, how much you are achieving, how everything seems to be working for you, how much you are loved or how much you love. In fact, rather than feeling a void or empty you feel full. When I feel like this, I am full of me, I am "Soul-ful", (full of soul).

How often do you have these feelings? This question may help you think about how much you are in touch with your "Soul".

Remove your barriers - take a fresh view on life

The more you are in touch with your "Soul", the less you are concerned to meet the external criteria, the fewer the barriers you feel you need to maintain, the more you are able to just be your "Self". When you are like this your "Soul" is in "the World" with your boxes open. You can receive all the information from it without the filters and you can give your "Soul" to "the World" without the need to control your behaviour.

You may think that to live like this would be too dangerous, that without protection you will be damaged. If that is so, you have the choice to use your barriers or not. But this will then be your choice, rather than an automatic response. We have seen that we often automatically follow patterns of behaviour which we do not check out and which may not be appropriate; remember "going to Sunday lunch".

Now You Can Choose

Having explored some of these questions you may now be beginning to see how in touch you are with your "Soul" and what is getting in the way. We have seen how the closed boxes are self-perpetuating barriers, how they prevent our self-development, and how they prevent us showing our true selves. If you have looked into your gold boxes you now have a clearer picture of yourself.

Having read this far, you may be concerned that this book will conflict with your existing knowledge, beliefs or values. You may be concerned that models you currently use to make sense of the world will be destroyed. This was our concern too, so the book is a series of thoughts and suggestions. You can choose what you take and when, so that you can integrate new ideas, concepts, and models into your life when and if they are right for you.

We do not intend to tell you what you should do. Wisboroughs let you look at what you do, how you do it and why, so that you can choose to change if you want to.

CHAPTER FOUR

YELLOW SHEETS

If having read this far, you would like to review regularly, this chapter will help you set up a routine. Yellow Sheets is probably the simplest way to re-view and is therefore a good place to start. To help you decide on your routine we shall describe how we first came across Yellow Sheets and how we have since adapted them for a variety of uses. You can then choose, and adapt to suit yourself.

How Yellow Sheets Developed

We first discovered Yellow Sheets when Richard was working with a friend on a short communication skills course where these reviews were built in. We introduced the idea to a six month management module of a social work course. We were working with mature students who were attending college one day a week. They worked as managers of day care units, homes for elderly people, children's homes, special schools and managers of care staff in the community. They managed between two and sixty staff.

At the beginning of the weekly meeting with the group we would hold a Yellow Sheets review. The students thought about the previous week's workshop, and how they had applied the learning at work. They also identified other learning from their work during the week. They individually wrote notes on yellow sheets of paper. To begin with, we gave the students a structure to help with their review. This later became unnecessary.

We originally only asked the students to write down what they had found most useful about the previous week's workshop, and how they had applied it during the week. Later on we developed this to include other things which they wished to review. For instance, someone may have had a meeting with his boss which had gone particularly well and he wanted to look at the reasons why. Or someone may have had a difficult supervision session from which she wanted to learn.

The sheets were yellow so that they were different from the other notes the students had in their files. Thus, they could easily identify their reviews over a longer period of time. They could see how well they were developing their skills. By only using one sheet each week the notes were kept short, and only included things which were important for some reason. They did not have time to re-read their lecture notes and discover what they should be remembering!

Using Yellow Sheets at Home and at Work

You might like to write your own Yellow Sheet now. Take five minutes to think about the last week and write a list of anything you remember which is important to you. Although our example is from work your Yellow Sheet may not be. It may be about any aspect of your life during the last week. It might include conversations with your partner, decisions you have made at work or at home, how you dealt with a rude shop assistant or carried out an appraisal at work.

From this list, notice what you have learned, make a note or circle the appropriate words on the list. Decide what you want to follow up as a result of taking this five minutes to think. You may be surprised how much you have learned without realising.

The social work students divided into groups of about six to discuss what they had written. This discussion generally lead to questionning for clarification, listening to other points of view and discovering that there were different ways of applying the same theories. They also realised that different things were important to different people.

They learned a lot from seeing how other people had applied something which they had perhaps thought was relatively unimportant. Following a workshop on assertion Corinne had taken the idea of personal rights and during the week had applied this in all sorts of ways at her place of work, a day centre for people with learning difficulties. She had looked at the rights of managers, careworkers, clients and clients' relatives, and as a consequence had started to write a client's charter for her unit. This was very different to the main point of the workshop and to the way others had applied learning from the day. This prompted the rest of the group to look at using the idea in a similar way at their own workplaces. Thus, social work practice was significantly changed in a number of different settings.

If you want to use your Yellow Sheets in this way, you will probably find that by explaining your notes to another person, you will clarify your own thoughts. Your friend or colleague will probably give you a different perspective of your week.

Daily Yellow Sheets

On other courses, where we worked with people every day, we used Yellow Sheets daily. We usually began each morning by asking people to write a list of things they found important, interesting or useful from the previous day. These were not necessarily part of the actual course content. They may have included thoughts during a coffee break, ideas prompted by comments from others in the group, ideas which appeared overnight or an idea from a day-dream.

After five minutes the group were invited to share their notes, and these were collected on to a flipchart. It was important that people did not have to share anything which they didn't want to. This sharing prompted discussion about the previous day's learning in a similar way to the social workers discussions, but this discussion was often then used as the starting point for the new day's work and learning.

If you work as part of a team you could find daily Yellow Sheets very useful. Everyone starts the day's work understanding each other's perspective of the previous day, and difficulties or misunderstandings can be sorted out. We have found it useful to use Yellow Sheets at the beginning of a new day, rather than at the end of the old, as people have had a night to sleep on things and reflect. Having been away from the situation over-night gives an opportunity to stand back, re-assess priorities and be more objective.

One of the leading authorities on adult learning in this country, Alan Mumford, has used a learning log for a number of years. He tries to think about what he has learned from his day to day life and writes notes every day to record this. He admits that he doesn't always manage to do it!

Yellow Sheets encourage teams and families to reflect and learn from their day to day experiences. A culture of learning and development becomes established.

An Example of Adapting Yellow Sheets

Many professional organisations insist that their members take part in some form of continuous professional development. If you belong to a professional organisation, you may find Yellow Sheets useful to help you learn, realise how much you have learned and as a way of recording your learning.

Recently, we have introduced the concept to our local branch of the Institute of Personnel & Development to support their continuous professional development initiative. This has taken the form of asking individuals to complete a Yellow Sheet, on which questions have already been identified. An example of this is shown below:

Discussion Questions for Branch Meetings

Please think about your answers to these questions and discuss them with four - six people sitting near you. If you attend Branch meetings regularly, it is useful to form the same group at each meeting so that previous learning can be followed up.

What did you want to learn?
What have you learned?
How are you going to use this?
What opportunities in the next month will you have to practise this?
What else do you need to know?
How are you going to discover this?
How are you going to record this learning?

As you can see the sheet was to be used at the end of each branch meeting, following a presentation. We discovered that members found this exercise helped them learn from the meeting and think about how they could apply the learning in the workplace. How often have you attended a meeting and not thought about how to apply the learning?

We found that these discussions lead to further discussion about work problems generally, so that members began to find the branch meetings more useful. You may like to think how you could adapt this approach if you run meetings, e.g. a camera club, the local chamber of commerce, the Women's Institute, Neighbourhood Watch, a football team. You can, of course, also use this approach for team meetings at work or family meetings at home.

Identifying questions

To make most use of Yellow Sheets you may like to think about why the questions outlined above are important.

What did you want to learn? This question clarifies your reason for attending the meeting. If you are clear why you are there you will get the most out of the meeting. You may not have gone to the meeting to learn anything specific. It is still useful to be clear about why you did go, if only so that you use your time well.

What have you learned? You probably learned many things that you did not set out to learn from the meeting. For instance, what makes a good presentation, how two people are getting on, what makes you feel confident, or how you behave when you are bored.

<u>How are you going to use this</u>? This question is asked so that learning does not remain an intellectual exercise but becomes part of your way of living.

<u>What opportunities in the next month will you have to practise this</u>? New learning is often lost because it is not used quickly enough. You may have watched a person at your meeting asking questions and learned a lot about questionning skills. So, you may wish to set up opportunities to practise this. You could use teatime to ask your son about his day at school, ask a colleague how he got on at a meeting, or discover your hairdresser's views about new hairstyles. Alternatively, there may be things you have to do anyway which require the use of questionning skills. For instance, you may have planned a day of recruitment interviews. You can now identify this as an opportunity to practise the skills.

<u>What else do you need to know</u>? You may have been prompted to discover more about the subject or yourself.

<u>How are you going to discover this</u>? It is useful to think of different sources of information. We often use the same ones without realising that others are available or may suit us better. Some people find books really useful, while others are happier talking to people. Choose what is best for you or experiment. When you feel confident enough find out by actually doing new things.

<u>How are you going to record this learning</u>? Are you going to draw a picture, make a note on your p.c., keep a journal, or write it in your diary?

Keeping Yellow Sheets

This is probably a good time to stress the value of keeping some record of your reviews. You will notice that all the different ways of using Yellow Sheets require something to be written down. We think it is important that this is done individually, with individual thoughts and feelings being recorded, whether or not they are to be shared with others. This prevents "group think".

We have found it very useful to have something to review against, particularly over the longer term. It really is very encouraging to be able to look back and see how far you have moved over a period of time. This can be particularly useful when you are feeling really fed up and want to "chuck it all in".

As you can see from our example, you can devise whatever questions seem to be appropriate for you and your situations. As we said earlier, we often ask groups to just think about events, and then write a list of things that they remember, or that were important to them. Yellow Sheets can be as simple or as complex as you like.

Starting Your Yellow Sheets Routine

To round this chapter off, you may find it useful to spend five minutes writing a list of things that you remember about the chapter for some reason, significant thoughts that occurred to you, and anything else of interest that happened to you while you were reading.

If you can, share some, or all of these notes with someone else. Finally, jot a note about your discussion and your learning.

You could do this with each chapter you read, or each time you have a period of reading. You could also do this the next time you go to the theatre or the pub, or each day during the coming week. It doesn't matter how you do it at this stage. It is more important to get into a routine of reviewing what you do, and realise that it is easy. Try it and see.

CHAPTER FIVE

SPLATS AND HOORAYS

Splats and Hoorays became our family's way of reviewing regularly; our way of learning from day to day events, and our relationships. They became a way of life.

Splats & Hoorays differ from Yellow Sheets as they introduce feelings and conscious judgements. "Splats" are events or people we would like to splat. "Hoorays" are events or people we are pleased with. We can work out why we view specific situations or events as either good or bad. You may find that Splats & Hoorays can be a more useful way of reviewing relationships than Yellow Sheets.

Using Splats and Hoorays With Your Children

How Philip used Splats & Hoorays

Chrissie first started talking about Splats and Hoorays with her son, Philip, as a way of helping him talk about difficult issues. Originally, Splats were things that he could imagine doing to people who had made him unhappy. It was a way of putting abstract feelings and thoughts into a concrete form. Later Splats became bad or negative things that had happened to him during his day and we added Hoorays to give some balance. The hoorays were good things that had happened.

Chrissie and Philip used to talk about Splats & Hoorays as Philip was going to bed. Chrissie had recently left Philip's father and now lived with Richard. Philip needed to sort out his feelings about everything and everyone.

Splats were a way of helping Philip free up, and express his feelings. At that stage it helped Philip discuss his negative feelings about Richard, his father and Chrissie. He could splat all the grown-ups. These negative feelings about us could come as a natural progression from any negative feelings about school, friends, etc. It is easy to admit to negative feelings about teachers at school. It is much more difficult to admit to negative feelings about your Mom. Splats and Hoorays helped Philip to do this.

Philip realised that it was worth expressing his own views, including negative thoughts and feelings. Chrissie tried to make sure that she didn't contradict, or deny him his feelings, or defend her actions.

This was also good for Chrissie as it meant she had to think about how Philip saw the actions of the grown-ups involved. She then had a new perspective on her own and everyone elses behaviour.

Having looked at Splats, we discovered that it was important to look at Hoorays as well. Otherwise only the negative aspects of the day were thought about. This would have meant that the review would have been a negative, unenjoyable experience so that Philip would not have wanted to do it. Re-living the good things about the day encouraged Philip to enjoy his good feelings as well. It also provides a balance so that he realises that every day has its ups and downs. That's life.

As we have said before, there is as much to be learned from positive experiences as negative ones. Children sometimes don't realise this as reviews only take place when they have done something wrong. Many of us grow up believing that learning is about pain and struggle. Reviewing positive events helps children realise that learning can be fun.

When to do Splats and Hoorays

We did Splats and Hoorays at Philip's bedtime each day as it was a quiet time together without distractions. The activities of one whole day was a managable amount of time to explore. If left for longer, little Splats could build up. Hoorays would go unnoticed and so be lost as part of positive experiences. The negative feelings could be dealt with, wrapped up and left behind before going to sleep. The slate would then be clean. There would be no negative feelings left over to colour the next day's events. Philip was then free to enjoy, learn and grow from the new experiences of the next day.

If positive feelings are recognised, they can then be stored and drawn on at will.

Using Splats and Hoorays to talk about feelings

We all have feelings, both positive and negative and these do not make us good or bad people. Often children are given the impression that it is wrong to have negative feelings such as anger, sadness, fear, or boredom and so they never learn how to deal with these emotions.

Splats and Hoorays was a way of helping Philip express negative feelings safely. He knew that he would not be disliked or judged because he had them, or because he sounded negative.

We know, from our own experiences, how damaging it can be to carry guilt for having angry feelings. You may remember feeling angry towards your parents and then feeling bad about it. You probably thought it best to tuck the anger away. Unfortunately it is still there inside you. We use a lot of energy keeping such feelings tucked away, and are unaware of the effect they are having on our behaviour today.

If we do not learn how to deal with all our emotions, issues can not be dealt with and relationships cannot develop. Children need help with negative feelings such as guilt, fear of a person, anger towards someone, anger with themselves, shame, etc. Splats is a safe vehicle for expressing such feelings. This can then lead to discussion about the emotions and help the child explore ways of dealing with these feelings. The child can begin to think about what he wants to do about the situation. He can begin to realise that he has some power and can actually affect situations. Children and grown-ups often have more choices than they realise.

Some people need help to enjoy good feelings. You may feel guilty if you are having a good time; particularly if you are surrounded by doom and gloom. It is useful for children to re-live the good experiences and the feelings that went with them, so that they can learn to enjoy these feelings. Having identified enjoyable experiences, a child and his parents are able to set up situations to ensure positive feelings can be found more readily. At the simplest level, if you discover that your child enjoys swimming, you can take her swimming. If a child knows what she enjoys it helps her to establish her own identity, and be more aware of herself.

If children are unaware of their feelings, or think that they should only feel certain emotions, it will limit their experiences of life. We can't live life to the full if we can't feel joy completely. In the same way, we can't grieve and leave a loss behind if we will not allow ourselves to feel deep sadness. We are unlikely to make dramatic changes in our lives unless we are spurred on by real anger or passion or pain.

What Happens to Your Feelings

Classifying emotions as either good or bad not only affects how we feel about expressing them, it determines if we will even allow ourselves to have them. If we feel very strongly that we should not feel anger towards our parents, we may not get as far as feeling guilty about it. We will simply not allow ourselves to have the feeling of anger in the first place. We will persuade ourselves that we are not angry at all. Richard has realised that he learned to feel sorry for himself, rather than feel angry.

Some men believe that it is wrong to feel sad (this may be an extension of "big boys don't cry"). This could mean that whenever they feel sadness coming on, they will make jokes about the situation or clown about. While this might make it easier for some people around them to manage, their inner self is still feeling sad, and storing the sadness away. The assumption that people find it easier may be wrong. It may make them uncomfortable as the man's behaviour is inappropriate in the circumstances.

For example, when Linda, a colleague of Richard's, broke her foot, her husband couldn't manage his feelings of serious concern. Having spent three hours at the hospital, Richard delivered Linda home in great pain and with her leg in plaster. Linda's husband made a joke about it.

On the other hand, quite a lot of people think that it is bad to feel happy. They don't think that it is wrong for other people to feel happy, but they won't allow themselves to. Whenever there is something to be joyful about, they will look for what could go wrong, what the bad bits are, why it won't ever work or how they can give it to somebody else.

Perhaps you've made one of these comments when someone has paid you a complement, "Oh, it wasn't really very good.", "Fred can do it much better.", "He did all the work really.", or "I don't expect it will work if I do it."

How do you classify feelings?

You may like to classify the following list of feelings for yourself by putting a   under the column of either Good or Bad.

Feelings	Good	Bad
Angry		✓
Joyful	✓	✓
Destructive		✓
Afraid	✓	
Excited	✓	✓
Hate		✓
Self-pitying		✓
Frustrated	✓	
Passionate	✓	
Loving	✓	✓
Bored		✓
Vulnerable		✓
Cowardly		✓
Lonely		✓

Splats And Hoorays

Feelings	Good	Bad
Compassionate	✓	
Creative	✓	1
Sad		2 ✓
Ashamed		✓
Embarrassed		✓
Brave	✓	
Depressed		✓
Aggressive		✓
Anxious		✓
Empty	3	✓
Impulsive	✓	.
Enthusiastic	✓	
Helpless		✓
Inferior		✓
Self-conscious		✓
Sensual	✓	
Powerful	✓	
Trusting	✓	
Stressed		✓
Successful	✓	
Happy	✓	✓
Guilty		

Add any others you think of

Which of these do you feel guilty about having?

Depressed
guilt
Anger
Self pity

Are there any of these feelings which you never have (e.g. some people never feel sensual)?

This exercise has probably shown you that there are some emotions which make you feel uncomfortable. You may also have noticed that you are aware of experiencing a group of feelings regularly, but that there are some you rarely experience.

Using Splats and Hoorays With Your Partner

We later extended Splats and Hoorays to regular daily and weekly reviews for us, as well as Philip. Again, it helped us keep sight of the positive things. It raised trivial issues early so that we would put them on the agenda for discussion. Without this we would probably have ignored many issues, thinking them too "silly" to mention. These would have festered until they were dragged up in some future row. We've all had a row with a partner and found that a list of gripes from the past ten years has suddenly appeared from our mouths as a list of accusations!

How we used Splats & Hoorays as a couple

We found it helpful to write our Splats and Hoorays lists separately, then come together and read our lists to each other before discussing them. There was no pressure to read everything. We did, in fact, as it was a good, safe way of sharing our perspectives of the day or week. Our lists of Splats and Hoorays were simply our individual perceptions. Neither of us had to defend what we had written. It simply opened up possibilities for discussion.

We often realised that the other one had a different perception of an incident. One of us had, perhaps, seen it as a much more or much less important event than the other. One may have seen it positively, while the other had seen it negatively. This has lead us to a much greater understanding of each other and of our relationship.

This morning Philip asked if he could wear his trainers instead of his school shoes. Richard saw this negatively because he thought that Philip was bucking the school rules. Chrissie saw the same situation positively because she was pleased that Philip had asked assertively and was trying to be more independent.

Having classified our feelings about the incidents of the day into Splats and Hoorays and shared our perceptions, we could now look more deeply into why we had these feelings and perceptions. For instance, Chrissie may have felt guilty about not doing something which she believed Richard wanted her to do. She may have been carrying this Splat around with her all day but then, having raised it in the evening, discovered that Richard did not want her to do this at all. So, Chrissie could now consider why she had believed Richard wanted her to do it and why she felt guilty about not doing it.

We have discovered that Splats and Hoorays emphasises our separateness as individuals because we are more aware of having different opinions and perceptions. Sharing our perceptions about ourselves and our relationship ensures that we take joint responsibility for the relationship.

Something which regularly features on our Hoorays lists is "Going for a walk on the Downs, by the river, by the sea, etc." It is good to remind ourselves of the pleasurable feelings we enjoyed during the experience. If you tend to have negative thoughts about your life, listing Hoorays like this one will help you become more aware of the positive experiences.

On the Hoorays side we felt good when Janet, our next door neighbour, knocked on the door yesterday to say "hello". We hadn't seen her for a long time. The questions, "why do we feel so good about it and why does she seem to like us?" led into a discussion about our expectations of other people.

Using Splats and Hoorays at Work

As development consultants, we further extended Splats and Hoorays into our work in organisations. We use it to help people in organisations review their work and relationships. Again, it is a safe way of exploring feelings which affect the way people do, or do not, work together successfully.

When Penny reviewed a day recently, she classified a meeting she had had with a colleague at work as a Splat. She was surprised that she had negative feelings about this meeting as she thought she had managed it well. We asked her why she thought she had negative feelings. She realised that it was because her colleague had been critical, and had projected her own anxieties about herself and her behaviour on to Penny. At the time Penny had accepted these as her own. If she had not reviewed she would have continued to feel bad about herself and would have behaved negatively with her colleague.

During the same review Penny identified her Hoorays. She was pleased that a member of her team had said he was delighted with the way he had completed a task she had given him. This lead us to discuss how her trust in him had developed and why she had encouraged him to take more responsibility. She considered her patterns of behaviour and feelings about risk-taking when delegating to staff.

Splats And Hoorays

Teams can use Splats and Hoorays

If teams discover that using Yellow Sheets works for them, using Splats and Hoorays on a weekly basis will help them look at how the team works together. Splats and Hoorays make it feel safe to talk about perceptions and emotions.

First, members of the team write their own lists of Splats and Hoorays. They then share them with the rest of the team. Sharing is emphasised so that no one takes up, or defends a position. When using Splats and Hoorays with teams, we always ask the question "why". For instance, if Fred's list of Splats shows he felt angry with me during a discussion, we need to work out why he felt angry. It would be destructive to ignore it or aggressively defend my position.

Teams have to be courageous to work in this way but they can initially work with Splats and Hoorays at a relatively superficial level. As the team becomes more confident and feels safer it can tackle more difficult issues. Members of teams who can learn to be honest with one another are generally much more success-ful as a team because they become more understanding and supportive of one another. Positive discussion and planning can come from regular reviews of a team's Splats and Hoorays.

Doing Yesterday's Splats and Hoorays

Take five minutes to write a list of your Splats and Hoorays for yesterday.

Share it with someone. You may not want to share all of them at this stage.

Ask each other these questions. If it is not possible for you to share your list with someone ask yourself the questions and note your answers.

- why did you think of the points on your Splats list as negative?

- why did you think the Hoorays were positive?

- why did you think particular things were so important?

- do some experiences appear on both your Splats and Hoorays list? Why do you think you have included them under both headings?

- has your perspective of any events changed while writing your lists and if so how and why?

- what do you now understand about your own feelings and actions and the feelings and actions of others involved in specific events?

- how do you feel now about yesterday and today?

and finally having written your lists and answered these questions:

- what have you learned?

- what will you do differently tomorrow?

What Now?

If you do daily Splats and Hoorays for a time, you will probably see that patterns begin to emerge. For instance, you may find that your Splats tend to be all around work, or a particular person, or your children. All your Hoorays might be about being out of the house, or with a particular person, or carrying out a specific activity. These patterns give you an indication of what is making you happy and what is making you unhappy. You can then decide what you want to change, how to go about it, and how quickly you would like to bring about any changes.

We have used Splats & Hoorays to work on the following issues:

Learning about ourselves and how to change

Being a more successful & effective team

Becoming more self motivated

Unblocking ourselves and others

Reducing our stress & being healthier

Being less afraid

Being unafraid of our feelings

Understanding our feelings and their effect

Being free to express our feelings

Growing through joy rather than struggle

Taking more control of our lives

Being more insightful of ourselves and others

Being more aware of the different aspects of ourselves

Becoming more honest with ourselves and others

Knowing what we want and being able to get it

Developing successful relationships

Developing self confidence

Accepting and loving ourselves as we are

We believe that you can use Splats and Hoorays to help with other issues but this list includes issues which are most obviously suited to a Splats and Hoorays approach.

Now you know that you can do Splats and Hoorays you can work out how to use it to explore your own specific issues.

We think that Splats and Hoorays is a quite simple but very effective way of reviewing. It helps, not only with our thoughts about events, but also with our feelings about them. It gives us an opportunity to explore and discuss our feelings with other people. We find that Splats and Hoorays changes our view of specific events, but even more usefully, it changes our perception of our lives.

CHAPTER SIX

THE FIVE STEP PROCESS

The Five Step Process is a Wisborough to change your perception of events and problems. You will re-view in several different ways and have a structure to plan your future action. You can use it to review specific incidents, such as a one off meeting, a particular presentation, a row with your partner or your child fighting with another child at school. It can also be used to review and solve a problem, such as failing to get reports in on time, never delegating work, shouting at the children, or getting angry with your partner.

We have found the Five Step Process useful to work with teams which display destructive conflict. Such conflict often arises from a number of unresolved incidents. As it is a structured approach, the team can explore these incidents in a safe way.

Again we would stress that it is important to review events you feel positive about as well as those which have left you feeling negative.

Slow down

We need to slow down the review process when we are exploring events. Often, when reviewing a specific event, we make value judgements about other people, ourselves, and the outcome. These come from a tangled mess of thoughts; what I think of myself at the time, what I think about other people, and my feelings. We rarely stop to examine the evidence, particularly if we are feeling very emotional about the event. If we do stop to look at the evidence, we do not ask ourselves what may be colouring our view.

For instance, Richard's ex-wife phoned last night and told him that his fifteen year old son, had been hurt in a fight after school. Richard's view of the situation was coloured by his feelings about his ex-wife, his feelings about his son, what he thinks about fighting, his view of himself as a father, as well as the information he was given. Unless he sorts out his thoughts and feelings any action he takes could be based on these thoughts and feelings, rather than upon any facts.

The Five Step Process gave Richard the opportunity to separately examine his thoughts and feelings as well as the facts. He could then see the influence of these before considering what action to take. He also recognised his current view of himself.

The Five Steps

Step One - Describe the event

Step Two - Share the description

Step Three - Clarify and challenge perceptions

Step Four - Identify personal learning

Step Five - Plan action to use and develop the learning

This chapter includes skills, and techniques such as questioning, listening, and planning. You may like to refresh your memory about these as they are an important part of the process.

We'll now look at the Steps in more detail.

Step One - Describe the Event

Your behaviour, thoughts and feelings

The first step is to describe the event or events over a period of time. This needs to be our own perception of the events; not what we think it should have been like, or how someone else saw it. At this stage describe the events in terms of "behaviour", "thoughts", and "feelings" separately. It will help you cover each area. These headings will give you a structure to begin your exploration.

Use "behaviour" to describe what everyone did or said at the time. We tend to select significant things to remember because they had an effect upon us. However, for now, we want to try to remember and simply record all the behaviour. Our interpretation will come later. If we start to interpret immediately, instead of simply recording, we begin to edit the information and are likely to miss useful data.

Having described the behaviour, you can now describe your thoughts and feelings. You will have had different thoughts at different times during the event and your feelings will have changed continuously. It is helpful if you can link these to what was actually happening at the time, i.e. what you and other people were doing. The links can be more easily seen if you use three columns and head them Behaviour, Thoughts, Feelings.

Separating thoughts from feelings

We often find it difficult to separate thoughts and feelings. When asked for feelings we may give thoughts. I may say "I feel that I was the quiet one in the group and didn't say very much".

This is a thought that I had at the time rather than a feeling. This thought may have made me feel sorry for myself or anxious but is not a feeling in itself. Because of this, it is a good idea to write your thoughts before you write your feelings.

Here is an example of a description of an event.

Behaviour	Thoughts	Feelings
Joan said she didn't like the plan.	The plan was my idea She is getting at me.	Hurt, angry
I said if you don't like it you can do it yourself	That will shut her up.	Powerful, Victorious
Joan looked at floor.	I have hurt her.	Guilty

Describing a recent event

You might like to use this format now to descibe an event which took place recently. When you have finished it check if you have confused thoughts and feelings. If you have found it difficult to identify your feelings, this is not unusual. Try to work out what they are by discussing with someone what you have written in the columns headed "Behaviour" and "Thoughts".

Using Gold Boxes to describe an event

You may find Gold Boxes useful to describe an event (see chapter 3). Use the headings:

- "The World" (your behaviour and knowledge)

- "Perception" (your interpretation of the world)

- "Values and Beliefs" (your values and beliefs about the people involved, the place, the event itself)

- "Self-Worth" (your feelings of self-worth at the time)

- "Soul" (how connected you were to your true self during the event)

Groups have found this very valuable if they want to look at a situation in depth.

Either structure encourages you to describe the event in several different ways; to break it down. This will give you a fuller picture, rather than focusing on only one aspect.

Step Two - Share the Descriptions

You can now share what you have written with someone or with a group. This sharing is a very powerful way of validating your experiences. This is especially important if the event has left you feeling negative about yourself. If we have had a bad experience we sometimes deny the facts and our feelings about the event. We still carry the negative feelings within us, but we hide them well. They will affect the way we deal with, or avoid, other similar situations.

Encourage empathy

While you read your description it is important that no one listening passes any comment or criticism. At this stage, your views should not be devalued or developed further. The listener could help you validate your experience by simply mirroring your feelings, e.g if the experience has made you sad, they might share your feelings of sadness. They could say, "that would make me feel very sad as well". Your views should not be added to, or taken away by comments such as, "it couldn't have been as awful as you have described", or "there, there, it will be alright".

You will find that you have to be clear in your own mind about what happened and what your thoughts and feelings were before you can describe the event to someone. Knowing that you are going to describe it, will encourage you to write a full and clear description. By verbalising your description, you will own your feelings about the event. They will seem more concrete. You will be able to examine them more easily.

If you are unable to share your description with someone you may find that reading your notes out loud can be equally effective.

If you are the listener

As we have already said, if you are listening to your partner's/colleague's/friend's description, try not to pass comments or criticisms. At this stage, your partner needs to be able to trust you and not feel that she is being judged. If she feels judged, she will want to defend or change what she has written.

You will find that if you start to judge, you will stop listening. You will begin to try to find solutions. Unfortunately, these solutions will be tailor made for you rather than your partner. You will be trying to find solutions without all the information you could have. You may also miss points which your friend or colleague thinks are important.

You can help your partner by

- listening for links between thoughts and feelings,

- listening for links between feelings and behaviour

- identifying connections and patterns

- hearing where there seem to be links missing.

For instance, if your partner said that she _felt_ upset about an event, but what she said she _did_ at the time, was deal with the situation in a humourous way, you can hear that there is a mismatch between her feelings and behaviour. This information will help you write your questions in Step Three.

Listening to someone's description uses all your senses. You watch what someone does while they are giving you their description. You hear the tones of voice and the emphasis that is placed on different words. If someone says that they were not worried about what happened, do they look and sound as if they are not worried? We often find that people say one thing, but we have a strong impression that they mean something else. This is more likely to be so when someone is talking about feelings. This doesn't mean that she is trying to deceive you; simply that she may be unaware of her true feelings. Here again, you will see your question for Step Three appearing.

While listening you may also realise that there appear to be huge chunks of information missing; whole stages of the event seem to have disappeared. Again this does not mean that the person is trying to deceive you but that there may be areas which she finds difficult to cope with. She may not have seen things because they did not fit her interpretation of the event. You can help with very sensitive questioning in Step Three.

Are you being heard?

Over the next few days you might like to observe when you feel listened to non-judgementally, when someone is interested in you, and when you feel you have not been heard. Try to make some notes about how you knew that you had been really heard. What did the person do and say while listening to you?

Step Three - Clarify and challenge perceptions

Step Three clarifies and challenges our perceptions, so that we can understand more about the event and learn from it. By writing your description you have debriefed yourself, and separated yourself from your original thoughts and feelings. You are now distant enough to explore what you have missed so far, why you behaved in a particular way, what your motives were or wonder why your feelings were so strong.

If you are the questioner

We clarify and challenge our perceptions by asking questions. We try to understand the event which the person is describing. Your clarifying questions help your partner understand more too. Your partner will see things in a new light by explaining the event to you in greater detail.

Clarifying questions are easy to write. Here are some examples. You can probably think of others.

"I don't understand ... . Please can you explain."

"How many people were in the room at the time?"

"Do you mean ... or ... when you say ...?"

"Wherabouts was she sitting?"

"What was he doing while this was going on?"

"Was that before ... or after ...?"

Challenging Questions

We also ask ourselves challenging questions to help us understand more about what happened and about our thoughts and feelings. As you discovered in Step Two, questions automatically appeared in your head while you were reading your description aloud. You may have realised that your explanation was not as clear as you thought, or recognised that you have been denying your feelings, or perhaps your reaction to the event was extreme. It is helpful to express these thoughts as questions to yourself to encourage you to search for answers which you may otherwise not see.

If working in a group, or with a partner, it is useful for each of you to write questions about your description. Everyone will have a different understanding of the original desription. Each person will bring different experiences, interpretations, prejudices and expectations and will therefore write different questions.

We have found that if the questions are written first, rather than simply asked, they seem to be more considered, have more weight and be treated more seriously. If each person individually writes questions, "groupthink" is avoided. Everyone has an opportunity to identify questions, rather than only the most vocal or the most powerful people in the group. The final value of writing questions is that you can take them away and think about them further.

We once worked with a group of managers who had a difficult meeting in which they had to decide if two of their colleagues could join the existing group for future meetings. The group had very strong feelings which were influenced by the closeness or otherwise of the relationships with the two colleagues. The following are some of the challenging questions the group identified during Step Three of their review of the meeting.

Some Step Three Questions

- Why did I want/not want Angela in the group?

- How honest was I about these reasons, thoughts, feelings?

- Why was I this honest/dishonest?

- How much do I actually know about anyone's real thoughts and feelings about this issue? How could I have discovered more? Why didn't I discover more?

- If this issue was important why didn't I raise it sooner?

- How did I contribute to the decision-making process?

- What are my hopes and fears about this decision?

- How happy was I with the decision? Do I want to do anything about this? If so, what and why?

- Following this meeting, how would I describe the level of trust/mistrust within the group? What is the evidence for this?

- What did I contribute to this state of trust/mistrust within the group?

- What is my perception of the group now? How has it changed?

- What new information did I get about individuals and the group from this experience?

Check your motives

The purpose of challenging questions is to help someone see more clearly. It is important to check that this is your real motive when challenging. We have worked in organisations where the culture of the organisation was said to be one of "constructive criticism". However, we often observed that managers had other motives for questioning. Some wanted to show how clever they were, others wanted to make someone look foolish, others wanted to score points or ingratiate themselves. Questioning can be used aggressively or manipulatively, rather than as a way to help or solve a problem.

If you have felt attacked or threatened at a meeting at work, or at a social function or by your partner, you have probably been asked questions in an aggressive or manipulative way. You may have then found yourself defending your position, rather than discussing your ideas further.

When writing challenging questions we are trying to help our partner feel safe enough to explore her thoughts, feelings and behaviour. If she appears to be defending a position we need to ask ourselves why and check out our motives.

Are you giving advice?

Open questions are often the most useful if you are trying to help someone explore an event further. If you look at the examples of challenging questions from the group review shown above, you will notice that they are all asking "why", "how" or "what". This helps the person stop and think, instead of simply agreeing or disagreeing with you. You will notice that the list above does not include statements, solutions or advice. By writing the questions you have a chance to make sure that they are helpful. If you hear the description and immediately start asking questions, you may find yourself making statements, finding solutions, or suggesting what they should or shouldn't do.

It is not helpful to write "why don't you do this?". It is less threatening and more thought provoking to write "why did you do it that way?" or "how did you decide what to do?" or "what else could you have done?". You can see from this example that the original question was actually advice in the guise of a question.

Asking Questions

Having written the questions, you can now ask them, and use them as a basis for discussion to clarify and challenge perceptions. You can help each other identify patterns of feelings, thoughts and behaviour. As the purpose of this discussion is to help your partner feel comfortable enough to explore the event you have to be aware of <u>how</u> you are asking your questions.

We have looked at the wording of questions, but the tone of your voice and your other non-verbal behaviour will give away your true motives. If you have made negative judgements, your partner will know this from your non-verbal behaviour. It will not match the words of your question. Your partner will become defensive.

While listening to the description you were trying to listen to the "music" as well as the "words". You are doing exactly the same when you are listening to the answers to your questions. These need to be discussed sensitively. Although you have a list of questions, each question will need time for follow-up discussion.

Funnelling

Follow-up can take the form of "funnelling". You start with a very general open question and gradually focus your questioning to a very specific point. We have laid out an example of "funnelling" on the next page.

If you finish with a summary, you can check that you have really understood what has been said. It gives your partner the opportunity to review what she has said and check that it is what she actually meant. It also helps you listen. You will listen more closely if you know that you are going to have to summarise.

The Five Step Process

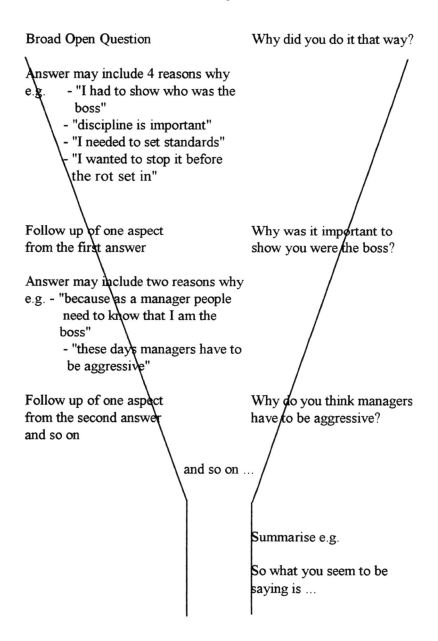

Broad Open Question

Why did you do it that way?

Answer may include 4 reasons why
e.g.   - "I had to show who was the
        boss"
      - "discipline is important"
      - "I needed to set standards"
      - "I wanted to stop it before
        the rot set in"

Follow up of one aspect
from the first answer

Why was it important to
show you were the boss?

Answer may include two reasons why
e.g. - "because as a manager people
        need to know that I am the
        boss"
      - "these days managers have to
        be aggressive"

Follow up of one aspect
from the second answer
and so on

Why do you think managers
have to be aggressive?

and so on ...

Summarise e.g.

So what you seem to be
saying is ...

The Cloud

Sometimes when working your way down the funnel you will come to what we have called a "cloud". This cloud is difficult to pass through because you are embarrassed, uncomfortable, or anxious about asking further questions. It may also occur because your partner is uncomfortable and doesn't want you to probe further. It needs sensitivity to decide whether to go through the cloud and continue with more probing questions, or to remain at a more superficial level. This will probably depend upon the level of trust between you.

Consciously make a decision at this stage, rather than continue with the funnelling because you think you are supposed to. Are you going to go through the cloud or are you going to bounce along it? As you are trying to help your partner, it is useful to remember that her needs are more important than your own at the moment. You need to be very sensitive to all the clues being given by your partner.

In the example below the speaker may have answered the question, "why do you think managers have to be aggressive?" with a long silence, shuffling in his chair and then said "well, you do, don't you?" This is when the cloud appears and is maintained by the questioner beginning to ask closed questions and making statements. For instance, "well yes, as a manager in your position I expect you have had to many times. Haven't you?" We call this bouncing along the cloud until you can safely find another subject for discussion. You will probably find yourself going on to the next question on your list.

If you want to go through the cloud you can either ask a "why" or a "how" question, e.g. "why do you say that", "how do you mean". You can also use a summary to help you both focus, and move the discussion on, either through the cloud or on to the next subject. You have made a conscious decision. You are not bobbing along the cloud trying to find a way to bounce off.

Funnelling Cloud

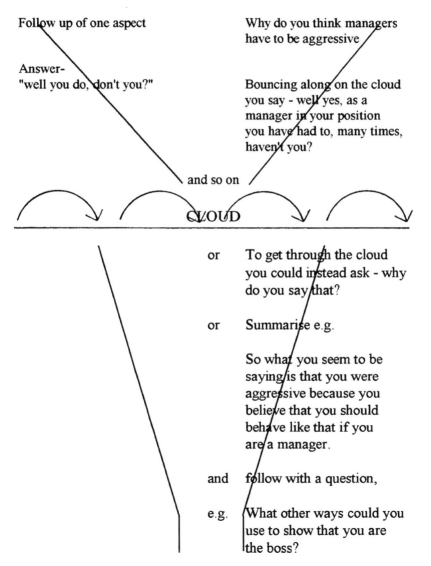

Follow up of one aspect

Answer-
"well you do, don't you?"

Why do you think managers have to be aggressive

Bouncing along on the cloud you say - well yes, as a manager in your position you have had to, many times, haven't you?

and so on

CLOUD

or To get through the cloud you could instead ask - why do you say that?

or Summarise e.g.

So what you seem to be saying is that you were aggressive because you believe that you should behave like that if you are a manager.

and follow with a question,

e.g. What other ways could you use to show that you are the boss?

Lists of questions

Once a discussion has started it is not a good idea to strictly follow your list. When funnelling, you will find that you have answered other questions on your list.

By the end of the whole discussion you should find that all your original questions have been asked and answered. The timing of the questions will be dependent upon your partner. If you ask your questions too quickly, or too deeply too soon, your partner may take fright. She will not be able to think and will begin to give monosyllabic replies. You will then find yourself unable to think and will respond to her answers with closed questions.

Funnelling all the time

Funnelling and listening so carefully may sound very difficult, but you do it quite naturally when you are interested in someone, or what he is saying and when you both feel comfortable. If you are genuinely interested in the other person and your motives are sound, you do not need to worry about technique. What we have been outlining here will simply help you improve your skills, or will help you when you feel anxious about questioning.

If you would like to practice funnelling, there are many opportunities to do so everyday. You may like to ask your friend about his ski-ing holiday, or ask a colleague about her project. As you can see, you can use the process to find out more about anything. While you are practising, you will find it helpful to notice when you reach a cloud, when you bounce along it and how you go through it. Notice also, how effective your summaries are and what happens when you use them in different places. If the other person becomes monosyllabic, ask yourself if you sound aggressive because you have asked difficult questions too soon.

The purpose of Step Three is to identify patterns of behaviour, thoughts and feelings, and to identify the connections between them. You need to remember that the discussion during Step Three is not an interrogation. If you challenge insensitively or too quickly it will sound aggressive and your partner will become defensive.

Be brave

During Step Three of your review you are trying to gain new insight and develop your thoughts and ideas. If you can keep an open mind and be brave, especially when you are asked difficult probing questions, you will discover so much about your perceptions and your values and beliefs.

Step Four - Identify Personal Learning

Record your learning

Following the discussion in Step Three, you can identify your personal learning and insights from your review. You can write yourself some notes about this. By writing notes you will become more aware of how much you have learned. This, and the deeper understanding of yourself, can help change a negative situation into a positive one.

You will often be able to re-frame so that your perspective of a situation changes. This will give you some control of the situation and help you see the choices that are available. You will probably be able to identify more choices from a new perspective.

For instance, a pattern Nick discovered from Step Three was that whenever he was spoken to in a pompous way he felt irritated. This had led him to dismiss whatever ideas Cliff offered. He realised that this was an habitual pattern which often determined his response in such situations. Having learned this, Nick can now choose how he would like to respond in future.

Writing notes will clarify and reinforce your new learning. As you have to find words to describe your learning, it will become more concrete and so you will want to take action. You can only work out what action you want to take with other people if you understand your learning and can talk to them about it. Finally, writing notes will give you the confidence to talk to others about your learning.

How do you learn?

Most people find it very difficult to answer when they are asked "what did you learn from that?". People learn in different ways, so they need to be able to identify their learning in several different ways. Kolb identified four different learning styles;

- learning from experience

- learning from observation and reflection

- learning from conceptualisation (using theories or seeing connections and patterns)

- learning from experimentation.

We all learn in all these ways but tend to have preferences for one or two of them, and so tend to learn more with these approaches.

If you prefer learning from experience you are likely to write your notes about your learning in terms of what you did or didn't do. If you like experimenting, you may find that your learning is written in terms of "good ideas" you want to try out. Alternatively, you may find that your learning tends to be in terms of observations (collecting data), or perhaps you show links, connections and patterns.

To discover how you prefer to learn you could write a list of the five most important things you have learned recently. Then describe how you learned them. Try to classify each description, using Kolb's four learning styles. Can you now see if you tend to have a preference for one or two of them? It is useful to be aware of your preferences so that you can consciously learn in other ways and expand your opportunities for learning. Your learning will not be restricted to only "doing" or only "thinking". If you are interested in learning styles we suggest you do Honey and Mumford's Learning Styles Inventory.

Using Gold Boxes to recognise your learning

Some people also find it helpful to structure their learning using the headings from the Gold Boxes model shown to describe an event earlier in the chapter. If you have used the model to describe the event the learning links can easily be made. The headings we used were:

- the World (behaviour and knowledge)

- Perception (interpretation of the world)

- Values and Beliefs

- Self-Worth

- "Soul"

You can ask what you have learned about other people, situations, and yourself in each of these areas. It is useful to check the evidence for this learning, e.g. how do you behave differently, what do you see differently, what beliefs have you let go, when do you feel you have more self-worth, what soulful experiences have you had?

We use this structure as it helps us recognise that our learning has taken place at a number of different levels. This is essential if we are to use our learning to bring about long term change. Again, you will probably find it easier to identify learning under some of these headings rather than others, according to your personal preference. You might remember that in Chapter 3, we mentioned Peter who learned how to be assertive (his behaviour in "The World") but could not maintain it over a longer period of time as he had not looked at his own "Values and Beliefs" or "Self-Worth".

Insights

You can now use your notes to identify the insights you have gained from your review. Here are some examples of insights people have gained from their reviews when using the Five Step

Process. We shall use some of these examples to help clarify each stage of Step Five.

"I tend to avoid situations where

- I have to meet new people
- make decisions
- take responsibility
- delegate
- give presentations".

"I tend to get angry when

- people use a dismissive tone of voice
- I feel nervous about a situation
- people don't understand me
- my boss tells me off publicly".

"I believe that people in that department think

- I'm a wally
- I'm too clever
- I'm too serious
- a woman/man should do this job".

"My reports to the production department are always late because I find it difficult to talk to women. So, I put off correcting the work of female secretaries".

Step Five - Plan Action to Use and Develop the Learning

Having used a structure to identify both your practical and conceptual learning, you now want to know how you can do things differently in the future. So, the final step is planning how to achieve this. There are many formats you can use to help you plan. Basically they all include the following questions.

Where am I now?

You have collected these insights during Step Four.

Where do I want to be?

Ideas for learning objectives will have come from your analysis and discussion, and can now be written in Step Five.

How am I going to get there?

This is your practical plan of action to meet your learning objectives.

As you have identified your insights during Step Four you can begin Step Five with ...

Where do I want to be?

You can use your insights to write learning objectives. Here are some examples of learning objectives developed from the insights shown in Step Four.

Learning objectives

If your insight in Step Four was "I tend to get angry when people use a dismissive tone of voice".

You could change it into one of the following learning objectives:

---

1. "To deal with my anger by ... " (e.g. asking questions, clarifying statements, expressing my feelings appropriately, etc.)

2. "To be more assertive when I feel angry."

3. "To explore why I feel angry when people use a dismissive tone of voice" (e.g. this may be because I was made to look stupid as a child, I believe I am not being heard, I feel superior or inferior to other people, etc.)

4. "To look at the effect my anger has on other people".

5. "To respect myself and others more".

6. "To find other ways of dealing with anger".

The first two learning objectives are behavioural and would fit into "the World" in the Gold Boxes model. The third can be seen in your "Perceptions" box. The fourth examines your "Perceptions", "Values & Beliefs", and "Self-worth". The fifth raises questions about "Self-worth" and the sixth could be explored in any of your Gold Boxes.

It is possible to write learning objectives to suit your current needs. You can choose how you want to explore and discover information about yourself. You can choose how to use this information. You can choose the degree of change you want to make in your internal and external world.

Even when the insight is purely about behaviour it is possible to have learning objectives at several different levels ("the World", "Perception", etc.). Look at the following examples and decide where you would place each learning objective.

Insight

"My reports to the production department are always late because I find it difficult to talk to women. So, I put off correcting the work of female secretaries".

Learning objectives

"To get my reports in on time".

"To be more assertive with women".

"To raise my own self-esteem".

"To explore my relationships with women".

"To check my perception of the female secretaries views of me".

"To clarify my views about women".

If you now recall your discussion, look at your notes about your learning, and the insights you have gained from your review, you can write your learning objective(s). You may find it useful to share this task with your partner, to help you clarify your objective(s).

How am I going to get there?

You can now plan how you are going to achieve your learning objectives. Your plan will include:

- how you will measure your success

- the opportunities and methods you will choose to use

- timescales

- any obstacles or difficulites you foresee, and how to overcome them

- names of people who can help you

- when and how you are going to review your progress.

Measuring Success

When carrying out your plan you need to keep yourself motivated and on course. You need success. So, before you start, you need to know what you mean by success. If you convert your learning objectives into objectives which can be measured, you can see if you have successfully achieved them. We often use numbers to measure objectives. You can quantify your success. You may think that this is impossible or too subjective, but we think it can be helpful.

When we worked with Freda, she believed that what she said was always dismissed by other people during meetings. It was not until she physically counted the number of times her views were dismissed and compared them with the number of times she was supported that she had the evidence to improve her self-esteem.

We'll take our previous example about anger and look at how the learning objectives can be converted into measurable objectives.

Insight

"I tend to get angry when people use a dismissive tone of voice".

1. Learning objective
"To deal with my anger by ... " (e.g. ask questions, clarify statements, express my feelings appropriately, etc.)

Measurable objective
This objective could become quantifiable by stating the number of times that I deal with my anger in my chosen way, e.g. "to deal with my anger by expressing it appropriately on four of the next six occasions I feel angry". You will, of course, have to decide for yourself what is "appropriate".

2. Learning objective
"To be more assertive when I feel angry".

Measurable objective
This could be written "to be more assertive three out of the next four times I feel angry". Again, you will have to decide for yourself if you have been "more assertive" than you used to be.

3. Learning objective
"To explore why I feel angry when people use a dismissive tone of voice" (e.g. this may be because I was made to look stupid as a child, I believe I am not being heard, I feel superior or inferior to other people, etc.)

Measurable objective
To make this objective measurable you could change the words "to explore why ...." to "to discover why ...". You will then be successful if you discover why and unsuccessful if you do not.

4. Learning objective
"To look at the effect my anger has on other people".

Measurable objective
This could become "during the next month I will observe and record the effect my anger has on Sue and Jane at work, and Bob and Sylvia at home".

5. Learning objective
"To respect myself and others more".

Measurable objective
This objective is difficult because it is about your deep feelings about yourself. It is probably an outcome of some of the behavioural objectives written above. To measure it you will need to know how often you feel self respect and what the circumstances are when you do or don't.

The objective could be written "after five incidents during the next two weeks I will reflect on, and record my feelings of self respect and the circumstances. In six weeks time I will repeat the process".

You will know that you successfully met your objective if you felt self resepect more often than during the first two weeks.

6. Learning objective
"To find out other ways of dealing with anger".

Measurable objective
This could become "to find four other ways of dealing with anger"

The examples above are very concrete, so that there is something to measure against.

There is no point in setting yourself learning objectives which are too difficult or in terms of "I should" or "I ought to". They will just give you another way to prove to yourself how useless you are. They will become self-fulfilling prophesies.

You may not be used to planning in such a concrete way. You can practise by taking your learning objective(s), and converting it into a measurable objective. Then, as you read each of the next stages of planning, work out ideas to suit you and your situation.

Opportunities and methods

Having identified your objectives, you now need to identify opportunities and methods to achieve them. There are opportunities in every situation for learning. People often don't see them because they have been taught to separate learning from everyday activities.

You can also create opportunities to practise or try out your new learning. When Chrissie was first interested in becoming more assertive, she used situations at work to practise her skills and be more aware of her feelings. She identified opportunities at work because it was safer than practising at home. We often need to look for such safe opportunities when we are trying to change, especially if those around us would prefer to maintain the status quo.

The methods you use can include anything, from reading certain books to meeting people, from talking with the children to going for a walk, from meditating to having counselling, from asking for a pay rise to starting a self-help group. Anything that you do in your life can be a method of development. If you identify the opportunity or method beforehand you will probably be able to take more learning from the event.

You will also find it helpful when you come to re-view your progress as it is useful to set out your expectations of success for each small step. It is too big a leap if change is only seen in terms of "here I am now and that's where I want to be in the future". If you give yourself signposts along the way, you can use these to hang your flags of success.

Signposts can signal your success or point you in a different direction to achieve your goal.

Timescales

Timescales in your plan will stop your good intentions leading to nothing. Your objectives become more real and solid if you consciously decide when to take action. You will also be more committed to the action.

While it is important to have a timescale which is tight enough to keep you on target, try not to be in too much of a rush so that you fail. The steps need to be challenging but small enough to be manageable. If you try to change too quickly you will probably fall back into your old patterns because you haven't built in enough reinforcement. You will then feel despondent and believe that you have let yourself down.

Appropriate timescales help other people around you manage while you are changing. You have probably met a woman who has been on an assertiveness course and immediately decided to change everything in her world at once. When she becomes disillusioned she leaves a trail of disaster in her wake. You may also have seen the new manager who sees himself as a new broom intending to make sweeping changes on arrival. There are similar results.

Obstacles and how to overcome them

Whenever we are trying to change we face obstacles. We have already said that people around you might not want you to change. Perhaps you want to change, but do not have the confidence yet. Both of these facts are obstacles to your learning and development. It is best to identify your obstacles before you start. Then you can begin to work out how to overcome them.

We have met many people who have worked out exciting plans to implement following a course. On their return to work they find that they were not given the time, resources or encouragement to carry them out. They were often surprised by this, and disillusion and disappointment added to their sense of failure.

Use the planning stage to look at your obstacles, and alternative ways to deal with them. When, or if, they occur you will then be ready to deal with them.

People who can help us

Obstacles can often be minimised or overcome by seeking other people's help and support before you try to take action. You may be surprised how much help you get by simply asking for it. If you are enthusiastic and sincere about your wish to change you will find that your enthusiasm is infectious.

We all need a friend

You need support when you are changing and developing. This support may not come from people involved with the change. You may find it helpful to ask people in a different setting for support. They will have a different perspective. Whoever you ask, you need to be able to trust them and they need to care about you. So, it is useful to build into your plan regular meetings or discussion with your support person, people or group.

At some time, everyone, working or learning on their own, suffers from a lack of support. Support means different things to different people and it is a good idea to work out your own list of what you need.

The support I need

This list might include:

- help to learn from my day to day work/life
- help to make connections between different life experiences, e.g. work, home, social, etc.
-   help to identify patterns of feelings, (e.g. when I feel confident/ anxious/ angry, etc.) and their effects upon my behaviour
- help to manage the needs of both family and work
- help to apply theories to practice
- offers of different perspectives
- someone to listen
-   challenges to test any conclusions I have drawn from my learning
- help to transfer learning from formal courses and different work experiences

- someone to look after the children so that I can think
- help to plan new experiences and opportunities for learning
- help with gaining support from other people and the organisation
- someone to compare notes with
- help to manage the needs of the job and my learning needs within the organisation's or the family's constraints.
- someone to pamper me and make me coffee when I feel a mess.

Support shows that others value and are interested in your learning and development. It will help to keep you motivated.

Having identified what support you need, you can now identify who can help you with what, e.g. your family, friends, your boss, your colleagues, your staff, and others like you in other organisations. Your plan needs to include how you can build up a support network, and how you will explain to people what you want and why.

Sometimes, you may think that you can't ask for support. Remember that you are offering something as well. For instance, your colleagues may learn from their discussions with you, your boss may understand more about your work and will be able to see a difference in the way you work, your friends may be closer to you, your partner may discuss issues with you more calmly. Everyone will understand you more.

Reviewing

This is the last stage of Step Five. As you have converted your learning objectives into measurable objectives you can now use them to measure your progress and success. When writing the plan you need to consider when and how you are going to review your progress. If you don't set reviews in your plan you may not notice that things are slipping. This may lead to you giving up, or falling back into old behaviour without noticing. As, throughout this book we have shown the importance of reviewing, it isn't necessary to stress its importance further here.

Your plan simply needs to show when you will review and with whom. You have already identified people to help you. You may decide to review by yourself. This is often the way, if the action you have taken is fairly simple. At other times you may want different people to review different parts of your planned action. For example, your spouse or partner for a regular weekly review or a work colleague following an interview with your boss.

When to review will be determined by the nature of your planned action. You need to review regularly if the final outcome is likely to take a long time to achieve. Small reviews on a regular basis will keep you motivated. When you do not feel very confident about dealing with a situation differently, you will want to review immediately after the event.

Finally, you will review the total plan to look at if, and how, you have achieved your learning objective.

All these reviews can follow some form of the Five Step Process. How detailed your review will be, depends on the stage of the review in the total plan. The final total review will be in more depth than those at the signpost stages throughout the plan.

You might now ask yourself the questions on the following page. (We have shown which steps of the Five Step Process they each refer to.)

STEP	PROCESS	USEFUL QUESTIONS
Step One	Description	- What was my objective?
		- What action have I taken?
		- What action haven't I taken?
		- Which objectives have I achieved?
		- How have my objectives changed?
Step Two	Share	
Step Three	Clarify & challenge	-How far do I think I completed the right objective
		- Why have I taken longer or less time?
Step Four	Insights & learning	- What have I learned?
Step Five	Planning	- What do I want to do now?
		- How?

And so, the process starts all over again.

"The Five Step Process" needs practise to use with ease. Now that we have outlined it, you can probably think of situations you can re-view over a period of time. Some of the examples we have used in the chapter may help you identify experiences you would like to review and learn from.

CHAPTER SEVEN

CONTRIBUTIONS

Here is a Wisborough to re-view:

- your family's life each month

- your team's development over a period of time

- a project you or your team are doing

- your personal development over a period of time

- the progress of members of a review and development group.

"Contributions" looks at what, and who, has contributed to your achievements. You begin by looking at what has been achieved and what has not been achieved. You then explore what and who has contributed to your achievements and non-achievements. This will lead you to plan for the future, accept responsibility for it, and be committed to your success.

We'll explain how "Contributions" works by describing a day's review with a committee of six people which had lost its way on a project. We have chosen this particular group, as we think that many of you will recognise the similarities with groups you belong to, such as the local tennis club, a project team, a school governing body, a firm of solicitors, a church committee, etc. During this day's review we looked only at concrete issues.

We shall also describe our work with a team who wanted to use concrete issues to explore how their relationships affected their day to day work. Finally, we shall look at how a family can use "Contributions" to review the ups and downs of their lives during each month.

The Contributions of a Committee

The committee was formed to identify a profession's post qualification training needs, and the provision to meet these needs within three counties.

The committee consisted of six people who were representatives of colleges and local authorities. They came from different counties and, although they all worked in the same field, they only met as a group for this particular project. They had been meeting about once every six weeks for almost a year. They had appointed a Chairman and a Treasurer.

We were asked to work with this group because they recognised that there was no longer commitment to the project. They were unsure how to to reach an outcome, or even what the outcome might be. They were not going to meet the deadline of an interim report in three months time.

Where to begin?

The day was to start at 9.00 a.m. The level of commitment of the group was demonstrated by the fact that only three of the committee had arrived by 9.00 a.m., and the last person didn't arrive until 10.00 a.m.

During the first session each member took twenty minutes to answer the following questions:

- what do you think the committee has achieved to date?

- what do you think the committee has not achieved to date?

- what and how do you think you have contributed to the committee's achievements?

- what and how do you think you have contributed to the committee's non-achievements?

These questions were asked so that every individual could see that the committee had achieved something and that they had made a contribution. This helped them feel that the committee might be worthwhile after all.

The questions raised issues of non-achievement. The feeling of non-achievement was no longer a vague feeling of anxiety. The anxiety became manageable when the issues became concrete, as the non-achievements were clearly identified. They could now be turned into achievements.

By asking each person these questions, the individual's thoughts were focussed on themselves as individuals and the committee as a whole, rather than only focussing on what other committee members had not done. This prevented the usual blame/attack syndrome which often occurs within a group which has lost its way. Working individually stopped members thinking defensively. They could look at the issue as a problem which the committee needed to resolve.

This format decreases anxiety and raises the level of safety within a group. It does not lead to complete trust within the group, but it does free people up enough to work on the problem. Issues of conflict can be looked at later.

Achievements and non-achievements

The committee then divided into two groups of three. They looked at each individual's lists of achievements and non-achievements. Each group came to agreement about the committee's achievements and non-achievements. The groups did not share their thoughts about contributions at this stage.

The discussion surprised and pleased the groups as they began to realise how much had been achieved. They shared good feelings and became enthusiastic. This put the non-achievements into perspective.

The discussion of the non-achievements encouraged people to share the original expectations of the committee. They began to understand other people's perceptions of the work of the committee.

A common purpose

Common themes and significant points about the committee's achievements and non-achievements were identified by the whole group. The group became calm and able to look at the problem constructively. There were common thoughts about what had been achieved and shared concerns about the future.

In this more positive frame of mind, they could use their lists of what had not been achieved to clearly identify the committee's purpose. When the committee was first set up the group thought that they had a clear purpose. This discussion showed that they had not shared it. Everyone had interpreted the objectives differently.

Contributions

The committee divided into two different groups of three. They looked at their contributions and again identified common themes and significant points. These were fed back to the total group. This was more difficult. The group could see how far objectives had not been achieved, because sufficient time and effort had not been given. However, this did not become a blaming or defending exercise, as everyone knew that the committee had achieved some success and that they had all contributed in some way to it.

Those who had contributed greatly realised that they had, and those who had not, saw how little they had done. As individuals came to these conclusions themselves, rather than being accused of lack of effort, there was no denial, but there was a feeling of gloom and doom.

The group now fully recognised its current situation. It needed to decide what to do and how to do it. The feeling of gloom and doom had to be lifted so that they could work positively towards this.

To gain some perspective, the group individually reviewed the morning. The gloom and doom began to lift as they realised how much they had learned from the morning. They were now ready for lunch and to move on to plan.

Contributions

Clear objectives

After lunch the group individually identified the objectives of the committee. These included their personal objectives and those of their organisations. They collated these objectives and categorised them. Discussion followed to gain agreement to a list of prioreties.

We asked the committee to do this work without us facilitating their discussion. This encouraged them to take responsibility again for their own problems and solutions. Teams become committed to planned actions if they take this responsibility.

Finally, the committee agreed the future action. They now knew which people had the necessary time, what resources were available and what degree of commitment they could expect from different individuals. The planning could be realistic and achievable, with everyone feeling that they could manage their personal workloads. There were no false promises.

No guilt

Most of the work was given to one person. They also gave him the money and the authority to carry it out. They agreed that he could make decisions on their behalf and set deadlines for them. The committee had recognised that this was the most practicable way to achieve their objectives. There was now no ill-feeling about an imbalance of workload, or guilt about not doing enough work.

What Have You Contributed?

You can see how "Contributions" was used to look at concrete issues with this committee. You might now like to use

"Contributions" to consider a personal project you are involved with, e.g. a team project at work, the jumble sale you are organising for next month, the school run you share, your personal development work over the last month, etc. We suggest you answer the questions on page 116. Then share and discuss your answers with someone.

Other contributions

You may now like to ask yourself:

- Who and what else has contributed to the achievements?

- Who and what else has contributed to the non-achievements? (In other words, "what were the obstacles to your success?")

We do not usually ask these questions until the first four have been answered. This prevents blaming and scapegoating and will encourage you to take responsibility for your own actions. Sometimes, people in a group will claim none of the responsibility for their success, while others will claim no responsibility for their lack of it. If people in your group are unwilling to take responsibility in this way, you may have to explore why, before you can move on to planning further action.

If you are working with a group of individuals who have different projects, or reviewing on your own, these two questions will help you recognise that other factors may affect your level of success.

For instance, you might recognise that someone is blocking your plan because they are not confident of the outcome. If you want their help, you need to identify this. Once you know what the problem is you can explain why you think your outcome is likely to happen.

You can now summarise your learning and make appropriate plans.

Using "Contributions" to Explore the Way A Team Works

As we have said, the extra two questions can lead to people looking more deeply at the idea of taking personal responsibility for the outcomes of the team, rather than blaming others. This may also lead to exploring the effect of personal responsibility on the way the team works together. A day we spent with another team will illustrate this.

A management team of three from the service sector asked us to help them review and improve the way they worked together. We had worked with them a year before, in the way we described with the committee, so they were familiar with our approach. They usually met together once week. They wanted to use a review of concrete issues to explore their relationships with each other so that they could work better together in the future. This was important because the decisions they made individually had an effect upon each other's work.

The first part of the day was carried out in the same way as the committee's day. We also included the previous two questions. This led on to the following questions:

- What can you learn from your contributions in terms of:

    - the effect on the achievements and the non-achieve ments on the service we provide?

- the effect on the achievements and the non-achievements of the management team?

- the effect on the achievements and the non-achievements of our staff?

- What is stopping you contributing more?

- How can we do things differently?

Power and control

The team then shared their answers to these questions so that they could again look for common themes and significant points.

This discussion raised issues about each individual's personal contributions. It encouraged people to identify and safely admit feelings of possessiveness of roles. Ruth discovered that she was keeping the decision-making process and consequently the power for herself. She had become the recognised decision-maker in the team and was concerned about the consequences to herself, if she let this role go.

Jonathan and Margaret had appeared to be happy for Ruth to take this role but had, secretly, often resented not being involved.

By now, the group trusted each other and wanted to solve problems. Ruth was able to explore why she was afraid of giving up her role. Jonathon and Margaret were also able to explore when they were happy to give Ruth this role and when they were resentful.

They also tackled other issues, such as fear of confrontation, wanting to be liked, and polarisation (their problem of polarisation is described on page 15 of the first chapter).

Later in the day the group identified their individual learning from each aspect of the day. From this, learning objectives were identified, so that they could be integrated into the normal plans of the workplace. Learning could then take place as the team worked towards concrete objectives back at the workplace.

The team began to plan how to meet the concrete objectives, identified from their achievements and non-achievements. They also began to plan how to meet their learning objectives about roles, confrontation, polarisation, etc. Their plans for the future had become team plans, rather than individual plans.

The team were now able to take away fresh ideas and objectives to complete their planning at their next meeting at work.

"Contributions" and The Family

Taking responsibility

You may remember, from Chapter five, that Splats and Hoorays can lead to individuals taking responsibility for themselves, instead of expecting others to take responsibility for them. Splats and Hoorays also emphasises joint responsibility for the relationships within the family.

"Contributions" takes Splats and Hoorays further by giving each person in the family an opportunity to see how they contributed towards their own Splats and Hoorays. When you identify your contributions you accept responsibility for them; for the things you feel negative about, (the Splats) and for the good things that have happened to you as well (the Hoorays).

Airing feelings

"Contributions" encourages you to explore how each individual contributes to the family's achievements (Hoorays) and non-achievements (Splats). By looking at how you believe each family member has contributed to the non-achievements, you can discuss different perceptions about guilt and blame. You can air feelings so that the feelings are not left to grow and explode later. You can all share the glory of the Hoorays. It is less likely that one person will feel that the good things have nothing to do with him. Also, whoever made something happen can have his contribution acknowledged.

Have you ever felt "miffed" because Dad (or Mom) took all the glory for an enjoyable family outing? You know that the day wouldn't have been so good if you hadn't planned the lunch, and the children hadn't helped with the chores before you went out.

"Contributions" would help everyone see why the day was so successful. It will become more enjoyable because everyone will remember how they contributed to it, and are responsible for its success. "Contributions" may also show that the day's success was a result of people's positive attitudes. The lessons from the review will help you have another good day out next time.

Sulking on Sunday

Sunday was not very good in our house that day. We were not getting on.

We looked at how we had all contributed to this miserable day. We discovered that Chrissie had decided to set her personal boundaries and stick to them. Richard and Philip had sulked. They had not been able to do what they wanted to, because of the bad weather. They had tried to blame Chrissie for their negative feelings. Chrissie would not take this responsibility. She would not find them interesting things to do, give up her activities, or get sucked into their "fed up" feelings about the day. Richard and Philip had stamped about, watched T.V., punished themselves, by working outside until they were frozen, and complained of being bored. You might recognise this scene!

We concluded from our review, that while Richard and Philip were sulking, they could not enjoy what they were doing and missed opportunities to do other enjoyable things. We learned that much less of the day would have been wasted if they had identified and expressed their disappointment and anger earlier, instead of sulking. Chrissie could have helped by pointing it out sooner. So, we agreed to help each other, by pointing out when we thought one of us was sulking, and helping each other come out of it.

Two days later, we had the first heavy snow for a long time. Philip wanted to stay home from school. He couldn't. He sulked. We talked about this at breakfast, so that Philip was aware that while he sulked he was missing the opportunity of enjoying the snow before school. He and Richard were then able to go out and enjoy clearing the snow together before Philip went to school.

Avoiding fixed roles in the family

Families who use "Contributions" to re-view regularly are less likely to fall into the traps of polarisation and fixed roles.
If you use "Contributions" with your family, you can discuss these problems in the same way that Ruth's team discussed their roles.

For instance, you can explore how roles can be shared by the whole family, rather than being given to one person.

Everyone is an individual made up of many parts. No-one is completely bad or completely good. We simply choose and are encouraged to take on some parts more than others. We become labelled "the star" or "the caretaker" or "daddy's little princess" or "the scapegoat".

Families often identify someone to carry the family's problem. This person becomes the scapegoat who may well be bad at school, drop out, fight, be alcholic or act out in some other way. Similarly one person may become the family hero and be admired and hardworking, successful at everything they do. By taking on a role, you may take it on for the whole family. This means that the others do not have to take the parts you have been given. Nor do you have to take their parts.

If my little brother is "the scapegoat" in my family, I do not have to be bad or even recognise those parts of myself. If my Dad is "the star" I may never be allowed to succeed. The family will never recognise that I have done anything well. If I have been given the role of "the caretaker" I will have to take the responsibility for making sure that everyone in the family feels o.k. So, I always have to cope and am never allowed to have problems of my own.

You may like to think what roles are taken in your present family or in the family you came from.

How to do a monthly re-view with your family

If you and your family would like to use "Contributions" to do a re-view of the last month we suggest you use the following format. You can, of course, adapt it to suit yourselves. The most important point to remember is to be honest, and not take up positions or defend yourselves. If you feel the urge to attack someone, stop and think, listen and ask questions. (You may like to look at Chapter Six on The Five Step Process to remind yourself about questionning and listening skills.)

1. First individually write answers to these questions:

- what do you think the family has achieved this month? (e.g. sorted out the disagreement between Fred and Rita, went swimming and enjoyed it, got the kids settled into school after the holidays, made plans for Grandma coming to stay, decided the rules for how tidy James' room had to be)

- what do you think the family has not achieved this month? (e.g. Mom still not being helped with the housework, the cars are still filthy, Mom and Dad still disagreeing about having someone come to do the gardening, we still haven't decided what to do on Dad's birthday)

- what and how do you think you have contributed to the family's achievements? (e.g. listened to what Fred and Rita had to say - asked good questions, didn't sulk when everyone wanted to go swimming and I didn't, gave extra time to the children after school during their first week of term, offered to give my room up to Grandma for her visit, asked James what he thought the rules should be)

- what and how do you think you could have contributed more to the family's achievements? (e.g. could have confronted Fred more about his behaviour, could have offered to collect Grandma from the station, could have helped James tidy his room)

2. Now share your first two answers and come to some agreement about your family's achievements and non-achievements during the last month. Record these.

3. Share your answers about contributions and together note common themes and significant points. (e.g. we all need to listen more, we tend to avoid confronting issues early enough, we've all sulked less this month, we seem to use James as a scapegoat and his room as an excuse to get at him, the children want Grandma to come but Mom and Dad don't, Mom was a martyr again sometimes this month, we all recognised that we didn't help Mom enough, we would like Mom to let us help her in our own way).

4. Individually write answers to the following questions:

- What have I learned from my contributions? (e.g. Listening is more important than I thought it was, it isn't so terrible to do something, like swimming, when I don't really want to do it, hadn't realised that Dad finds it so difficult when his mother stays, need to look at why I give James a hard time, realised when planning Grandma's visit that I enjoy planning)

- What is stopping me contributing more? (e.g. I'm too tired and have done too much this week, I didn't have enough time for myself last week, I'm having a hard time at school this term, I don't feel confident enough to confront Rita at the moment)

- How can I do things differently? (e.g. I could help Mom not play the martyr by asking her what she's got to do that day or what she doesn't like doing, I could listen to James' worries about school more, I could try to explain what I'm thinking more often)

5. Share your answers to these questions. Discuss your perceptions and help each other identify personal learning.

6. Discuss and decide what you want to achieve next month, both personally and as a family.

7. Write notes about what you want to do and what you want to learn.

8. Work out how you are going to help each other do this.

For instance, if you decide that you want to go to the zoo, decide how and when you will go. What you want to learn might be how to help Dad enjoy himself more when he is out with the family.

We see the purpose of the family as being to help children become whole, individual, well balanced adults and for the adults in the family to either become or maintain themselves as whole, individual and well balanced. This needs the family to have healthy relationships and a healthy way of living, physically, emotionally and spiritually. You can use "Contributions" as a family to re-view your relationships and lifestyle to see if it is meeting this purpose. You can then positively plan how to keep on track to meet the family's and individual needs.

What would you like to keep & what do you want to change?

"Contributions" is a good way of raising the consciousness of your team or family. Everyone will become aware of

- their individuality,

- their personal responsibility,

- their joint responsibilities,

- their relationships with others, and

- what is happening within the team or family system.

You can choose what you want to change and what you would like to maintain.

CHAPTER EIGHT

VISUALISATION

We use visualisations to re-view past experiences, gain new insights and discover new and often unexpected visions of the future. In this chapter we shall explain how you can use visualisations when you do a Wisborough.

What Is Visualisation?

Visualising is imagining ourselves in different situations. It is something you do all the time, consciously and unconsciously. Whenever you remember what happened to you in a situation, you imagine yourself back in time. When you listen to a radio play or read a book, your imagination creates the images for you to see. When you are planning the future, you use your imagination to see what will happen.

Visualisation not only allows us to see the pictures but lets us feel the emotions which situations generate. Sometimes these are emotions which we have been unaware of in our everyday lives.

When you use visualisation you are initially using your imagination in a focussed way, rather than simply daydreaming. You can then let it wander where it will in the situation you have created. You do not have to worry about having a good imagination or being creative. You do not have to worry about having clear pictures. Some people sense and feel things, rather than see them. To some people sounds and words are more important. You can't get a visualisation right or wrong. It just is. So, we have found it very useful for Wisboroughs.

Uncovering Thoughts and Feelings

You will find visualisations useful for Wisboroughs as they help you explore thoughts and feelings, as well as specific behaviour. As we have said, people often find thoughts and feelings the most difficult part of re-viewing. Visualisations help to unlock feelings, particularly for those people who are very good with words and know all the "right" things to say. Chrissie can often fool herself about her motive for doing something but visualising may show her the real motive behind her actions. She has sometimes been surprised!

Our motives are often mixed and it is difficult to discover which is the driving one. For instance Jane believed she was helping Steve develop by giving him responsibility. However, she was also punishing him because he had upset her by not taking enough responsibility previously. So, she unconsciously made the task too difficult and he failed. Jane was then confused because she hadn't been able to help Steve develop. Jane hadn't identified all her motives. She had only identified the positive ones. We often keep our negative feelings hidden, even from ourselves, and it may be these feelings which motivate our behaviour. Using a visualisation to review afterwards can help us understand what happened, as we begin to get in touch with our feelings at a deeper level.

Discovering Values and Beliefs

If you have a general feeling of unhappiness, but can't identify the cause(s), a visualisation will help you. It could help you see the cause(s) at a number of different levels. If you remember the "Gold Boxes" model we showed in Chapter 3, you will recall that we talked about different levels of consciousness affecting our behaviour. We showed that our behaviour in "The World" was affected by our interpretation ("Perception") of the world and our use of our "Values and Beliefs", as well as our own "Self Worth". When trying to review we sometimes find that we get stuck at one of these levels. For instance, we may not be able to identify our "Values and Beliefs" and so cannot see how these are affecting our "Perception". We can use visualisation to put us in touch with our "Values and Beliefs" and the effect they are having on us in a particular situation or with certain people.

Doug said how pleased he was that his wife was now working and had started a new career but he was actually making it quite difficult for her. He knew that as a "modern husband" he should be encouraging her. He was confused when it was pointed out that his behaviour was inconsistant with his words. He used a visualisation to help him understand, that locked inside him, was the belief that women should stay at home and raise children.

He was unaware of this belief because of his thoughts about what he should do as a "good" husband.

Having discovered this hidden belief, he could then decide what action he wanted to take. He could work on a number of different levels, e.g. he could look at where his beliefs about women come from, and work on changing those. He could change his behaviour. He could choose what he wanted to work on.

Re-viewing Relationships

When you review relationships at work or at home it is often difficult to see what is going on because you are so closely involved. You can use a visualisation to re-live a scene in your relationship and then explore with someone what happened during the incident.

Problems with the boss

If you are having problems with your boss you can use visualisations to help you review the situation and plan what you want to do about it. For instance, You may find it difficult to think about your relationship with your boss because you are very anxious whenever you meet him, or perhaps even when you think about him. However, because you believe that you should not be so anxious, you hide these feelings from yourself and others. You probably can't explain what your relationship is with your boss. You just know you don't look forward to meeting him. If you only review by thinking about your meetings with your boss, you may well use logic and rationalise away your true feelings. You will be able to explain your behaviour and your boss's quite logically, but you still will not look forward to meetings with him.

If you visualise yourself in a meeting with your boss, you will be able to see how you behave and you will be able to get in touch with the feelings you have during your meetings. Having identified what actually happens, you can decide what you want to do, e.g look at:

- how you behave,

- what effect your perception of the situation has on your behaviour,

- what effect your "Values and Beliefs" about bosses has on your relationship, or

- how your feelings of "Self Worth" affect the relationship.

You may want to work on some of these, rather than only trying to change your behaviour with your boss. As we have said before, if you only work on changing behaviour it may be difficult to maintain the change.

Visualise a scene with your partner

You can also use visualisations to review your relationships at home. Chrissie helped Tony, a client she was counselling, visualise a conversation with his partner, Sarah. Tony visualised himself asking Sarah some questions about her behaviour towards him. He also told her about his feelings. Afterwards, when Chrissie asked him what had happened, he suddenly realised that during the whole of the visualisation, Sarah had not listened to him. He recognised that this was a reflection of what happened whenever they tried to talk about their relationship. Tony realised that this was the reason he was so angry with Sarah, and that his anger about this had stopped him discussing problems constructively. Having become more aware of his anger and the pattern of their conversations, Tony was then able to explore this specific aspect of their relationship and decide what he wanted to do about it.

How To Do a Visualisation

As this technique is new to many people and sometimes people are anxious about using it, we try to introduce people to the idea by firstly giving them a simple, enjoyable experience. We'll explain a little about the technique and then give you an opportunity to try a visualisation for yourself before you read any further.

We often begin and finish a visualisation in a garden as it can be a warm, safe, familiar and comfortable place. However, we also use other warm and familiar places, such as a place we go to on the Downs, a path in the woods, or a room in a house. Although we have said that these places are familiar they are not necessarily real. They can be created in your imagination. It is useful to remember that whatever happens in the visualisation, you can always return to this safe place.

It is important to relax to slow down the mind and free it from its usual activities. Some of you will now be saying "but, I can't do that. My mind is always full". Don' worry about this. When you are visualising you can just let the thoughts come and then let them go.

Your mind needs to be free from its usual chatter to allow the visions to form. We find that focussing on breathing is very helpful as it slows you down, and frees your mind from your usual thoughts. We concentrate on breathing at the beginning and the end of a visualisation as it provides a link between what is happening in your vision and in the real world.

We sometimes find it helpful to have gentle repetitive music in the background. At the beginning of a visualisation this helps slow the mind and body down and at the end of the visualisation, it helps you become aware again of what is going on around you.

The following exercise will probably take about five or ten minutes. We suggest that you ask a friend to read the instructions to you or that you read and record them on to a tape first. You need to pause long enough throughout the visualisation to allow the pictures to form and to become totally aware of the experience, so that you can have the feelings which come with the experience. Where you see ... in the instructions we suggest that you pause for ten to fifteen seconds. Later on, your experience will tell you if these pauses are long enough and you can adjust them accordingly.

When you have finished your visualisation you will probably find it useful to write notes about it, including notes about your feelings at different stages of your visualisation. We have already said quite a lot about taking notes in previous chapters, so you will know that this will help you get the most from your visualisation.

If you have asked someone to read the instructions to you, you may find it useful to talk about your visualisation with that person afterwards. If you are using visualisation with a group, it is useful for everyone to write notes and then share these in twos and threes.

We have found it very useful when working as a couple to have Chrissie read Richard the instructions and for him to share his visualisation notes with her. Then Richard reads the instructions to Chrissie and she shares her notes with him. We have discovered a great deal about each other by using this technique, and have been able to help each other gain new insights.

In the following instructions you will see that we often go through a gate in the garden wall. In different visualisations we make different journeys through the gate in the garden wall. We have already mentioned two of these, i.e. Tony and Sarah's conversation, and going through the gate into your boss's office. In this chapter you will find other journeys you can make.

Instructions For a Visualisation

First, relax, sit in a comfortable upright position with your feet on the floor and your hands resting easily in your lap ... Have your shoulders relaxed but straight ... Have your head upright and straight. Make sure that both the left and right side of your body are balanced ... Close your eyes and gently become aware of your breathing ... Be aware of your stomach going in and out as you breathe slowly and gently ... If thoughts drift in, have them and then let them go ... You may like to count slowly to four while breathing in and then gently to four again while breathing out ... Continue this for three or four breaths, being conscious of your breathing or your counting ... Feel your body getting heavy ...

Now imagine yourself in a garden ... It is a warm summer's day ... Look around at the flowers and shrubs ... See the trees, notice the grass ... Is there any furniture in the garden? ... Can you smell the different flowers, the grass ... Be aware of the sun on your face and body ... Feel the warmth ... Look and see what you are wearing ... Listen to the sounds ... Can you hear birds, insects, the wind through the trees, perhaps some running water .... Walk further into the garden and enjoy looking, hearing, smelling and feeling ...

Now, notice a wall at the end of the garden ... Walk towards the wall ... See a gate in the wall ... Look at the handle on the gate ... Reach out and open the gate ... Go through ... You are in a pleasant place, you may find that you are in a field, on a hilltop, in a wood, on a beach, in a favourite room ... Look around and notice where you are ... Notice the smells ... Look at the colours ... Feel the temperature ... Listen to the sounds ... Enjoy the sensations ... How do you feel? ...

Now turn around ... See the gate in the wall ... Walk towards it ... Look at the handle on the gate ... Reach out and open the gate ... Go through it, back into the garden ... Once again be aware of the warmth, sights, sounds, colours, smells and enjoy them ... Walk back through the garden to where you started ... Have one last look around ... Become aware of your breathing again ... Wiggle your toes and fingers ... Gently come back into the room and open your eyes ...

Now, take a few minutes to become aware of your thoughts and feelings. When you have done this write yourself some notes about your visualisation and your thoughts and feelings at different times during it. Then note your thoughts and feelings now. Share these with a friend.

Reviewing Childhood

You can use visualisations to look at how your adult behaviour is affected by events which happened to you as a child. Sometimes our reaction to situations is out of proportion to the actual situation. This may be because the feelings in the currrent situation reminds us of our feelings as a child in similar situations. In these situations, we were, often, powerless. As adults we have options available to us which were not available when we were little.

An example of this happening to Richard was when he received a letter from the headteacher of the school where he was a governor. Richard had been asked to write an article about the school and had sent a copy to the headteacher, out of courtesy. He received it back with a line through a section of it, comments on how it could be improved and a statement saying that "the rest was excellent".

Richard was furious, out of all proportion for the situation. He was reminded of being at school and having his work treated in a similar way. As a child he was unable to discuss it, and so felt powerless and frustrated. These feelings were triggered again by the headteachers's comments. As an adult Richard had to remember that he had the power to ring the headteacher and discuss his comments, ignore them, or ask someone else to write the article. He could choose.

It is not always as easy to identify the source of our over reaction to situations. Visualisations can help us identify where these feelings are coming from so that we do not have to react to situations in the same way as we did when we were five, or eleven or fifteen.

You can visualise yourself as a child and get in touch with the feelings that you had. You may even discover feelings that you denied yourself as a child, or have since failed to identify as an adult. Having identified and got in touch with your feelings, you can choose to express them so that they will not have such a powerful impact on your behaviour as an adult. You may use the opportunity to identify a negative situation from your childhood and grieve for yourself and/or others. This will help to also free you from its negative effect.

We have used visualisation to do "inner child" work to grieve and free us from painful experiences. It has helped us stop laying blame and take greater responsibility for ourselves as adults. It has released us to be ourselves, rather then small children trapped in adult bodies. The "inner child" concept gives us a useful way to be less afraid of our feelings so that we can use them to be truly in touch with ourselves. We have found John Bradshaw's book, "Homecoming - Reclaiming and championning your inner child" particularly useful.

As getting in touch with these feelings from childhood is very powerful and can be overwhelming, it is not a good idea to use visualisations in this way unless you have the support of someone who has already done this work. We would suggest that you use a counsellor or a therapist to help you.

What Are You Like Now?

We can use visualisations to find out what we think about ourselves now, and how we would like to be. Sometimes our thoughts about ourselves are confused by our "shoulds" and "oughts". They get in the way of us knowing our strengths. They colour our perception of ourselves. They block our self knowledge. Visualisations can free our view of ourselves from our "shoulds" and "oughts".

This next visualisation is one we have used with managers to help them discover what they really think about themselves, but this visualisation does not have to be about you at work. You can choose any situation you like. For instance, you might like to use it to think about yourself

- at home as a partner, or as a mother or as a friend, or as secretary of a club,

or you might like to use it to think about yourself

- at work as a colleague, or as a manager or in your professional capacity or as an employee.

If you haven't done any visualisation work yet we suggest you do the one shown on page 138 before doing this one. This is so that you will be comfortable with visualisation and the scene will be familiar to you.

For this visualisation follow the instructions on page 138 from "First relax ... to "Reach out and open the gate ... Go through ... " Continue with the following:

Now look around ... Notice where you are ... Notice the smells, the light and the sounds ... How warm is it? ... How do you feel? ... Be aware of how you are standing or sitting, notice your posture ... Listen, you can hear two voices in the distance getting closer and closer ... you recognise them, one is someone who knows you well and the other hardly knows you at all ... They cannot see you ...

As they get closer you can hear what they are saying ... They are talking about you ... The one who hardly knows you is saying what <u>they've heard</u> about you ... Listen ... ...

Now the person who knows you well is speaking ... They are talking about what, <u>in fact</u>, are your strengths and your limitations ... Listen ... ...

Now let the voices fade until they have gone ... How do you feel? ...

Now turn around ... See the gate in the wall ... Walk towards it ... Look at the handle on the gate ... Reach out and open the gate ... Go through it, back into the garden ... Once again be aware of the warmth, sights, sounds, colours, smells and enjoy them ... Walk back through the garden to where you started ... Have one last look around ... Become aware of your breathing again ... Wiggle your toes and fingers ... Gently come back into the room and open your eyes ...

Now, take a few minutes to become aware of your thoughts and feelings. When you have done this write yourself some notes about your visualisation. You may find it useful to answer the following questions:

- How did you look, move, etc.?

- How did you feel at different stages? Why?

- What do you want to remember or forget? Why?

- What did you discover about yourself?

- What are your thoughts and feelings now?

Now share your notes and discuss them with a friend or colleague. This discussion will probably take you a minimum of twenty minutes.

What Do You Want To Be Like?

When planning how we want to be in the future, we are often unclear about what we want. Visualising can help clarify our wants. A visualisation can unlock your unthought of vision of the future; desires that perhaps you hadn't dared to turn into thoughts. Richard and I did not see ourselves as writers. We refused to be academics and saw ourselves as practical facilitators of workshops. So, when people suggested we should write a book we continued to say that this was impossible. This book has only materialised because of our visualisations. We realised that we did have a hidden desire to write.

Your own limitations, expectations or beliefs of how the world is or should be, can get in the way. You can use a visualisation to explore what is preventing you achieving your view of the future. Richard had always held a belief that life should be a struggle. Therefore, everything he wanted to achieve had to have struggle planned into it. The task had to be made difficult. Richard discovered this while using a visualisation from Gill Edward's book, "Stepping into the Magic". He visualised his "struggler", and discussed with him why they had to struggle. Having discovered this, he now takes account of this belief and challenges it when he plans. Frequently the plan is made easier.

Before doing this visualisation to discover what you want to be like, make sure that you have done the previous one to discover how you see yourself at present.

Now follow the instructions on page 138 from "First relax ... to "Reach out and open the gate ... Go through ... "Continue with the following:

Now look around ... Notice where you are ... Notice the smells, the light and the sounds ... How warm is it? ... How do you feel? ...

You can see a person who is an expert, a wise person, who can use their own experience and deep wisdom to help you fully discover and believe in yourself ... Listen to what they say ... They are speaking clearly, explaining with enthusiasm, how you can use your skills, experience, qualities, and opportunities to fully discover and believe in yourself ... Hear what they say ... ...

Ask the wise person what is stopping you ... Listen to the answer ...

Think of a question you would like to ask the wise person ... Ask your question ... Listen to the answer ...

Now feel yourself becoming that wise person ... Realise that you are that wise person ... You have been listening to yourself ... How do you feel? ...

Now turn around ... See the gate in the wall ... Walk towards it ... Look at the handle on the gate ... Reach out and open the gate ... Go through it, back into the garden ... Once again be aware of the warmth, sights, sounds, colours, smells and enjoy them ... Walk back through the garden to where you started ... Have one last look around ... Become aware of your breathing again ... Wiggle your toes and fingers ... Gently come back into the room and open your eyes ...

Now, take a few minutes to become aware of your thoughts and feelings. When you have done this write yourself some notes about your visualisation and your thoughts and feelings at different times during it. You may find it useful to use the following questions:

- what did you feel at different times during your conversation?

- what did you learn from your conversation with the wise person?

- what can you now do to continue to discover and believe in yourself?

- What are your thoughts and feelings now?

Share your notes and discuss them with a friend or colleague. Again, this discussion will probably take a minimum of twenty minutes.

You can, of course, use this visualisation to ask your wise person whatever you like. It can help you realise what your true feelings or values really are about yourself, others or specific situations. You can also talk to your wise person whenever you want to.

These two visualisations were originally adapted from ideas in "Self Development" by David Megginson & Mike Pedler.

You can visualise your future by allowing yourself to see yourself in the new situation, living it successfully and enjoying it. If you are taking big decisions and responsibility for your future, this will remove some of your fears. It will give you a picture of how your life could be. It will make what you are aiming for more concrete. This will increase your commitment to your image of the future, and give you the confidence and energy to achieve your aims.

Feeling More Confident

When visualising, you can live through in your mind what your future could hold. You can safely explore different ways of achieving your vision. You have a means of trying out your plans to see which one will work best for you. You can foresee some of the difficulties which might occur with each different choice. This will help you make your choice. Having identified the difficulties you can now include ways of dealing with these in your plans. A colleague of ours visualised a client receiving a letter he had written to her. He watched her open and read the letter and saw her responses to each paragraph. He was then able to change the letter until his client responded positively to the whole of it. He then came out of the visualisation and wrote the letter.

If you would like to use a visualisation to rehearse a situation you have to deal with soon, you might like to adapt the following visualisation. It is one we have used to help people give successful presentations confidently.

Follow the instructions on page 138 from "First relax ... to "Reach out and open the gate ... Go through ... " Continue with the following:

You are in the room where you are going to make your presentation ... Look around ... Notice where you are ... Notice the smells, the light and the sounds ... How warm is it? ... How do you feel? ... See the faces of your audience smiling at you ... Go to the place where you are to sit or stand to make your presentation ... Look around at the room ... Look around at your audience ... See them eagerly waiting to hear you ... Start to give your presentation ... Hear yourself speaking ... Notice your audience's responses at different stages of your talk ... ... Begin to wind up your presentation ... Notice your audience's reaction ... Notice your feelings ...

When you have finished walk out of the room into a corridor ... Remember your audience's positive responses to different parts of your presentation ... How do you feel? ... Remember the parts of your presentation with which you weren't happy ... Think how you would like to change them ...

Go back into the room and give your improved presentation again ... ... Notice the audience's positive reaction to everything you say ... If there are still things you would like to change, go out into the corridor and do so ... When you have finished giving your presentation successfully stay and enjoy the warmth from the audience ...

Walk to the back of the room ... See the gate in the wall ... Walk towards it ... Look at the handle on the gate ... Reach out and open the gate ... Go through it, back into the garden ... Once again be aware of the warmth, sights, sounds, colours, smells and enjoy them ... Walk back through the garden to where you started ... Have one last look around ... Become aware of your breathing again ... Wiggle your toes and fingers ... Gently come back into the room and open your eyes ...

Now, take a few minutes to become aware of your thoughts and feelings. When you have done this write yourself some notes about your visualisation and your thoughts and feelings at different times during it.

If you have found this chapter on visualisation interesting we hope that you will enjoy using visualisations to explore your past, your present and your future. You can use visualisation whenever you like. Chrissie's son, Philip, sometimes likes to use a visualisation at bedtime. If you think about it, this is very similar to telling a child a bedtime story. We all like stories and can have our very own.

CHAPTER NINE

A BASKET OF GOODIES

So far, we've mostly used words to re-view our experiences. In this chapter we look at a range of different tools or techniques to re-view, many of which don't just use words. This could be a great release if you find words difficult to use or if you use words so well that they mask your true thoughts and feelings. These ideas are ways of getting round both of these problems. These ideas will also help you review more creatively.

Are you stuck?

You will find this basket of goodies is helpful when you are feeling stuck. When we feel stuck it is often because our thoughts and feelings have become blocked in some way. For instance, if you grew up believing that you shouldn't feel frightened, you probably started to block the feelings of fear. Now, when a fearful situation arises, you habitually think and behave in a certain way. You avoid having any feelings. This may prevent you reviewing a situation which you find frightening. If you can't get past the block to review the situation and change the way you deal with it, you continue to repeat the same patterns. If you find yourself having the same thoughts over and over again, these ideas may encourage you to think differently.

What about your team?

If your team or group feels very comfortable together and mildly bored by each other, it is probably stuck or blocked. Everyone has become used to the roles they have taken, know what each one is expected and likely to think and say, and so, comfortably carry on repeating patterns. You may collude to avoid any discomfort which might be caused if you have different thoughts, feelings or behaviour. Your team thinks that there should be no conflict. You may even be reviewing regularly but the reviews are always the same. The process and the outcomes are predictable. People have stopped listening to each other because they think they already know what everyone thinks. Ideas from the basket of goodies will bring about new perspectives and recharge your reviews. Your team will begin to move forward again.

When we have used these ideas they have sometimes worked well simply because they are a novel way of exploring situations and people are often surprised to find that they can use them so creatively. We think of them as a basket of goodies because we keep them in a bag which we carry around with us when we help groups review. We hope that you can take something from this basket when you get stuck.

Pictures

The first in our basket of goodies is the one we use the most. You can draw pictures when you are unable to express your feelings. You may feel confused or unable to explain what a situation feels like. For instance, when asked what the situation is like at work if you say, "I don't know", or "I'm not sure", try drawing a picture to represent yourself at work.

Sometimes we use Pictures when we can see that people's behaviour is not matching their words. They may be saying that everything is fine but seem very agitated. Sometimes people believe that they should say everything is o.k.

As we've said, we use pictures instead of using words. Some people find it easier to express themselves in this way and enjoy doing it. Others don't, if they think they can't draw, or if they prefer using words. However, we have always found it very useful, even if groups are reluctant at first.

It doesn't matter if you can only draw stickmen. You don't have to be able to draw to use Pictures to explore a situation. The picture is only used as a representation. It is not an accurate picture but it does lead to reflection and discussion.

Your view of yourself

You can use Pictures to re-view your view of yourself. If you want to do this now as an exercise, please follow the instructions as you go along. Cover up the rest of the page and don't read the end of the section until you come to it.

Firstly, take five minutes to draw a picture of a tree.

When you have drawn your picture, look at the tree and describe, to someone how it represents you. If there isn't anyone to talk to, write yourself some notes as if you were describing your picture to someone. You may, for instance, have drawn a picture of a Christmas tree decorated with lights, coloured balls and tinsel. You might say that this represents you as, having lots of "show", and glamour to cover up the fact your needles are beginning to drop because you feel in decline.

You may like to ask yourself these questions:

- how large have you drawn the tree and why?

- where have you placed it on the paper (e.g. is it central, tucked in a corner, squeezed in the margin, taking up the whole paper, extending beyond the paper, etc.)? Why?

- how have you drawn the branches (e.g. are they twisted, tangled, straight, reaching out, reaching upwards, sparse, etc.) and how does this describe you?

- what is the trunk of your tree like? Is it straight or does it lean? What does this say about you?

- how would you describe the roots of your tree and what does this tell you about yourself (e.g. are they strong enough to support you, deep enough to feed you, etc.)?

- is there any life nesting or living in or on you and what clues do you have about your life from this?

- what is the overall effect of your picture (e.g. is it blowing in the wind, is it square and sturdy, is it calm, rounded, gentle, spring-like, full, precariously placed, in the sun, in the rain, etc.)?

- is this how you see yourself, or how you would like to be seen or how you think others see you?

If you would like to alter your picture, do so. This will give you some clues about changes you would like to make.

Changing times

We usually ask people to take a piece of flipchart paper and some coloured pens, and take five minutes to draw a picture to represent themselves in a particular situation. Each one then shows their picture to the others in the group and explains what it means. Even at this stage people often see things in the picture which they hadn't realised they had drawn or which they hadn't originally intended to draw.

The group then comments on what they see in the picture and asks questions about it. The questions are to clarify, not to criticise. If you are not used to this process you may like to look at chapter six on clarifying and challenging questions in the Five Step Process.

Here are three examples of pictures drawn by people in a group we worked with, where the organisation was going through a period of change, and a number of jobs were to be lost. The title of the picture was, "How I see myself in the current situation".

You might like to look at the pictures, as if you were part of the group. What do you see in each one? What questions would you like to ask each person? What comments would you make? What feelings do they arouse in you?

What do you really want?

We sometimes use Pictures to help an individual or group discover how they would like things to be. This is a creative way of helping people to think before they are constrained by the structure of a plan. Having used pictures to begin a review, and having done some work to explore the issues involved in the situation, we might then ask a group to work together to draw a picture to represent how they would like the situation to be in the future. This encourages the group to talk together about how they see the future, what is important to them, what values they share and how these affect what they want to do. This can be done without having to worry about whether or not it is possible, or practical. It is, after all, only a picture of a shared vision. It is afterwards that people realise the power of that shared vision and that they have made a commitment to it.

During a programme we ran to develop managers as trainers, we asked the group to draw a picture to represent themselves as trainers working in the future. Roger's picture clarified so much for him that he decided he didn't want to be a trainer after all. This was very positive because it stopped him doing something which would have made him very unhappy and which would have probably caused damage to the people he would have had to train.

Roger's picture was of himself on a tightrope. This was his perception of his organisation's expectations of a trainer. It was only during discussion that he realised that, in his picture he had no safety net, that he was doing a balancing act, with no means of support, and that he looked frightened. He realised this was actually how he felt about having to take on the role of a trainer.

Confronting fears

Some other powerful pictures we have seen have been:

- a man, who was going through a divorce, drew a picture of his children locked in a house with his wife, while he was outside, trying to rescue them.

- a woman, trying to develop her own career and becoming aware of the pressures on her at home, drew a picture of herself buried beneath her house.

- a woman, who was very involved with her work, drew a picture of her children standing alone in the middle of the page and her husband's car going in one direction and her's going in another.

Using pictures to review in this way allows people to confront themselves with their fears about situations. They can now do something to deal with their fears and work to change their situations if they want to. Situations can only be changed if we are aware of our fears and if we recognise what we need to change.

The pictures we have just described were used to look at deep concerns people had at the time. As we've also seen in this chapter Pictures are often used to look at issues which may not be so dramatic.

Russian Dolls

We have a set of five different sized Russian dolls which fit inside each other. We use them primarily to look at relationships within a team or family. Individuals can use them to explore their perception of themselves, other people in the team and their relationships with each other.

To show how they can be used we will give an example of James, describing the way he saw his relationships within his family. He was eleven at the time.

James was trying to describe what it felt like when he lived with his Mom and Stepfather and how it was different when he stayed with his Dad. He was finding it difficult. He couldn't find the right words. We got out the Russian dolls, took them out from each other and gave them to James to use to describe the different situations. He chose the middle size doll to be himself when he lived at home with his Mom. He chose the biggest and the next biggest to be his Stepfather and Mom. We asked him which was which and he said that sometimes his Stepfather was the biggest and sometimes Mom was. We explored with him when each was the case.

Our discussion included views and ideas to do with the colours of the dolls, and their facial expressions, as well as their sizes.

For instance, James said that when he stayed with his Dad he became a smaller doll (the second smallest) and his Dad behaved like the second largest doll. He said that it was like this because his Dad thought that he had to behave bigger than he really was and this made James think he had to be smaller than he really was. James believed that when he was with his Dad he could only be eight. He said that sometimes his Dad changed from being the second largest doll to being the very smallest and needed looking after. He believed that his Dad sometimes acted big because he felt small.

As James's Grandmother was going to stay with them for a holiday, James introduced her as another doll and showed how big this made him and his Dad feel. When Grandma came to stay his Dad tended to became the very biggest, loudly coloured doll, and James felt even smaller in comparison. He said that he felt like the very smallest baby doll but did not become it. He tried to stay as the second smallest.

We continued the descriptions by moving the dolls about so that they faced each other, stood closer or further away from each other or knocked each other over.

James found Russian dolls a lot of fun and very helpful as it allowed him to understand for himself why he felt so different, and why he behaved so differently in different situations. We found it very illuminating.

Why do Russian Dolls work?

One of the reasons that Russian dolls work is that people have to make choices between the dolls. People will often say "well, I didn't really mean someone to be bigger than someone else".

Nevertheless, they made that choice, rather than another one, and can then look at the reasons why they chose to do it that way. Using James's example, we could look at when he thought his Stepfather was bigger than his Mom and then why.

It is very safe to move dolls about and talk about them as dolls instead of as people. Russian dolls work because people choose who they want the dolls to represent and move them about without thinking about their reasons. They don't work it out logically. It is only after the dolls have been moved around each time that we ask why particular dolls are in particular places or why particular dolls were chosen to represent particular people.

Russian dolls encourages people to get in touch with their feelings, rather than use their intellect to block their feelings.

As people become more comfortable with using Russian dolls and become more involved in the exercise they begin to give a running commentary of what they are doing and their reasons for moving the dolls. So, fewer questions have to be asked. In effect, individuals begin to answer their own questions.

Coins

We use coins to review relationships in a similar way to Russian dolls. We ask individuals to take a handful of coins of different size and value, and to then choose different coins to represent different members of their family or team. We then ask them to place one on a table, or the floor, and then place the others around them. It is important that people make their own choices and layouts before they then go on to describe why they have made them and how they think they reflect their family or their team.

A Basket Of Goodies

How valuable are you?

Coins work for similar reasons to the Russian dolls. It is different because the coins have different values, as well as size. This allows individuals to look at why different people are represented by coins of a larger or smaller value. They can explore what each coin's monetary value is being used to measure, e.g. If Carol is represented by a 50p piece and Derek is represented by a £1 coin this may reflect that, in my perception, Derek has more power than Carol. The values of the coins can be used to represent all sorts of things, e.g. the amount of responsibility, decision making, control, work, affection, etc. which individuals are perceived to give or take. This is a useful way of people discovering how they judge and value themselves and others.

What is happening in your team or family?

By laying out coins, people often discover clearly how their family or team works. Previously their ideas about how things happened may have been unclear. We often have a sense of how things happen but cannot explain what actually takes place. As with the dolls, the coins are chosen and placed, seemingly without thought. When people begin to describe why they have laid out the coins in a particular way, they begin to see the patterns of behaviour, beliefs and values of individuals, and the relationships between team members. The relationships can be examined by looking at how close different coins are placed to one another, as well as the value of the coins used to represent different people.

If you are working with your partner, a colleague, your family or your team, it is useful for each person to work with a handful of coins at the same time. So, each person simultaneously chooses and lays out their coins. Then each person takes it in turn to talk about their layout and what it means to them. Your partner, and others, if you are working in a group, can ask questions about why you perceive things in a particular way. After each person has had time to describe their layout and talk about it, it is useful to look at and compare the different perceptions of people and relationships.

The fact that coins have a value, gives an understandable measure to help compare different perceptions. For instance, if two people have used a £1 coin to represent someone in their layouts but a third person has used a 2p coin, there is a very obvious difference in the size, colour and financial worth of these coins. This will prompt discussion about what criteria was being used by each individual when choosing the coins and why the perceptions of that person are so different. You can learn a lot about your partner or your family or your team by using this exercise. They will also learn a great deal about you. It often helps people realise why there are misunderstandings about situations.

Have a go

You might like to try this exercise for yourself now. Simply take a handful of coins of different value. Choose a coin to represent each individual in your family, your team at work, your committee at the squash club, or any other group of people you have a relationship with. Remember to choose a coin for yourself. Lay them out flat in any way you like. Then stop and either explain to someone, or write notes to explain, why you chose each different coin to represent each person, and why you have laid the coins out in that way.

Notice which coins are very close together, if all the coins of a certain value are together, if any coins are placed a long way from the others, if there is a coin around which all the others are placed. Are they all spread out or are there any coins connecting other coins? Notice the value of each coin and what that means to you. Is the most important person in your group represented by the highest value coin, and if so, why? Who does the coin of least value represent, and why? You will probably think of lots of other points to note, especially if you are discussing your layout with someone else. Lastly, write a note of what you have discovered from this review exercise.

A suit of playing cards can be used in a similar way to coins. People choose cards, lay them out and share their reasons for their choices, as before.

Shells and Stones

We sometimes use a collection of shells and/or stones instead of coins. The only difference with this is that there is the added dimension of physical qualities such as smoothness, roughness, colour, beauty, sharpness, delicacy, shinyness, size, etc. These easily translate into personality traits or physical qualities of people.

People may feel more free to use shells and stones as they don't have the financial value of coins as a measure. The physical properties will give different values when people are choosing them.

For instance, Matthew chose a long thin razor shell to represent himself and placed this between a small blue mussel shell representing his father and a polished piece of rose quartz representing his mother. His shell was very close to both his mother and his father.

He chose a pair of matching cockle shells to represent Joe (his mother's partner) and his father's partner. Joe was placed next to "mother" on the same side and almost as close as "father". "Father's partner" was placed on "father's" side, some distance from "Matthew". Other more distant relatives were placed further away, also on either his "mother's" or "father's" side.

We could see from this, that Matthew saw himself as keeping his mother's and father's families separate. When we asked him about this we had a discussion about how he thought he had to keep the peace between the two sides by being close to both his mother and his father.

The discussion clarified for Matthew a great deal about his relationships with his family and helped him see what was happening to him. Once we all realised what role Matthew thought he should take we could help him realise that it wasn't always necessary or appropriate for him to take the role of peacekeeper.

Glove Puppets

A colleague of ours reviews situations by replaying them using glove puppets. Individuals can transfer their thoughts, feelings and actions on to the glove puppet. The puppet can speak on their behalf. It can say things which they could never bring themselves to say, perhaps in very exaggerated voices. They can not only say and show what they believe happened but can explore how they would like it to be different in the future.

By asking the puppet questions the person is free to use the puppet to say what he really thinks or feels, rather than what he thinks he should say. Other people in the group can also ask the puppet questions. The puppet is allowed to say things which the individual would not allow himself to say.

Puppets are very useful when reviewing with children, but adults find them a great release as they can really be themselves while using a puppet to represent them.

Musical instruments

Another colleague uses the concept of an orchestra being made up of different musical instruments. When a group is stuck while reviewing its relationships, he asks them to each choose a musical instrument to represent themselves in the group. They then discuss why they have chosen that instrument and what qualities it represents. Other people can then comment on how they see that musical instrument and these perceptions may be useful to the individual.

This method of disclosing your perception of yourself will free your mind of the usual words you use to describe yourself. The comments about different people's perception of musical instruments also helps free the group to have a deeper discussion than it may generally have.

If your group feels safe enough you can then move on to choose musical instruments for each other and discuss the reasons for your choices. It is important that the reasons for the choice include some examples of behaviour as evidence for the choice. For instance, I may choose a trombone to represent you because I think that you don't say much but that when you do it is loud and heard by everyone. I need to then back this up with examples, from specific situations, as evidence. People may be surprised that they are seen in a different way from the way they perceive themselves.

You might like to now think of a musical instrument which represents you in a particular group, e.g. your team at work, your family, your rugby team, your women's group, etc. Why have you chosen this instrument to represent you? Can you think of examples of situations you have been in which illustrate this. What instruments would you use to represent the others in your group? Again, why and what evidence is there for your perception? Even if you don't share this exercise with your group it could be a good way of helping you understand your feelings when you are with the group.

Animals

We have also been involved in groups, where animals have been chosen instead of musical instruments. Many people feel more comfortable with choosing animals, rather than musical instruments because they are more familiar with them and therefore can have more choice.

This idea works in exactly the same way as musical instruments. You may like to now think of an animal instead of a musical instrument and follow the instructions above to see if this idea is helpful to you.

Corners

You can use Corners with your team or a group to review their relationships. You will find it useful if the group has stopped developing, or trying to understand each other. You can also use it if your team has become complacent.

Corners encourages people to explore their perception of themselves within a group. It lets them check their perceptions with other members of the group. Corners also gives a safe focus for discussion of their perception of others in the group.

How to use Corners

When we use Corners we put up, in each of the four corners of the room, a different list of words and statements. The lists are covered up and at each stage one word or statement from each list is uncovered, so that there is one word showing in each corner. We cover the lists up by simply folding the bottom of the flipchart sheet up over the words and stick it to the top of the page with blu-tack so that it can easily be uncovered to show the first line of words, and so on.

Here are the lists for each corner.

Corner 1	Corner 2	Corner 3	Corner 4
Deliberate	Decisive	Questioning	Reflective
Persistent	Impulsive	Tenacious	Consistent
Angry	Gentle	Aggressive	Calm
Passive	Involved	Enthusiastic	Intense
Sparkling	Quiet	Brilliant	Animated
I speak first	I wait to speak	I wait to be asked	I see what others say first

I am an alienated member of the group	I am a postive member the group	I am an integrated member of the group	I am a marginal member of the group
I am authority	I fight authority	I run from authority	I recognise authority
I like to help others	I look after myself	I get on with the task	I want to be looked after

The group stand in the middle of the room and are asked to individually write which of the four words they think is applicable to them as a member of the group. When all the group has chosen an appropriate word, we ask everyone to go and stand in the corner displaying the word they have chosen. No-one speaks until everyone has taken their places in the corners of the room.

We then ask the following questions:

- are you surprised to find yourself in the same group as others? Why?

- are you surprised to see which corners other people have chosen for themselves? Why?

- where would you have expected to find other members?

- how do you feel being in the corner in which you find yourself?

- what does the word or statement mean to you and why did you choose it?

These questions prompt a great deal of discussion.

We then ask people to move to other corners if they would now like to change. Again, similar questions are asked to encourage further discussion.

Everyone then goes back to the centre of the room and the next set of words are uncovered. The group are again asked to individually write down their choices between the new four words or statements. The process continues until all the words and statements have been discussed.

We usually use Corners at the end of a day when we shall be meeting together again the following day. This gives people time to think about their thoughts and feelings over night. They have the opportunity to talk further about it, during a review, the following day.

We would only use Corners when a group had been working together with us long enough to feel safe with each other. Therefore, we would not do this on the first day we worked with a team. Corners will not work if the group does not feel safe enough to reveal their thoughts and feelings to each other. They will simply choose a word or statement which they think is safest in this group.

How am I seen?

Corners is very powerful because people have to physically move and take up a position. It forces people to make choices in the same way that they are forced to make choices with a multi- choice question in a survey. The words are often not words they would have readily thought of to describe them-selves. They may think that none of the words suit them or that they fall halfway between two. However, having to make the choice and physically move helps people sort out what they really believe their perceptions to be. They know they always have the opportunity to explain later.

For instance, we worked with one group where George chose "questioning" and "persistent" for his first two choices and the group agreed with him. However, his third choice was "gentle" and he was surprised to find that the rest of the group would have chosen the word "angry" for him. He was pleased to be seen as critical and questioning as he thought that as an engineer this was the way he was supposed to be. He didn't realise that his colleagues interpreted his behaviour as anger. His colleagues valued his questioning but did not like the way he did it, or his reason for doing it.

This exercise helped George realise that he was now free to ask questions when he wanted to, rather than because he thought he should as an engineer. With the support and understanding of the rest of his team, he could develop questioning skills which were more acceptable.

Different interpretations

People sometimes say that a statement is ambiguous and could have several interpretations. We ask people to choose a corner based on their own interpretation. This sometimes leads to two people standing in the same corner, for totally different reasons. This makes people more aware that there are always different interpretations of the same circumstances within the group. Corners brings these interpretations out into the open.

Corners may evoke emotions as people are being more honest with each other. This is useful as it helps the group realise that it can deal with emotions safely. This results in the group becoming more cohesive and willing to take risks.

You can probably now see why we say Corners is very powerful. We think that it is important that it is used only at the right time and with caution. If your group wants to use Corners choose your facilitators with care.

Sculpting

When we use Sculpting to review, individuals stand in a place which represents where they see themselves in a group in relation to others. It is similar to Coins which we have already mentioned but the people themselves take up the positions, rather than using a coin to represent each person in the group. It is useful because people do not just talk about their relationships, they use the space in the room to show how they see their relationships physically.

Some groups are very good at talking about issues but little seems to change. Sculpting makes the talk more real as people take up the physical position which they have been describing. Taking up the positions is like looking in a mirror and seeing a reflection of yourself and your group. It gives an opportunity to check out if what you are saying is a true reflection of what you really think and feel.

How are you placed?

Like Corners, it is powerful because it physically moves people around. Emotions are felt because of the movement and the proximity of other people. If you are a marginal member of your family and you are placed six feet away from everyone else you will feel the emotions raised by being a marginal member. The other members of your family will feel the emotions they have because you are marginal. The whole group will recognise the effects of your marginalisation. This will then open up the possibility of a much more honest discussion.

When everyone has taken up the positions someone has chosen for them, we ask:

- are you surprised to find yourself in this position? Why?

- are you surprised by other people's positions? Why?

- where would you have expected to find other people? Why?

- how do you feel about being in the position you find yourself?

Depending upon where their discussion of these questions leads, we can then ask people to move to other positions if they would now like to change. Again, similar questions can be asked to encourage further discussion.

As with Corners, you need to choose your facilitators carefully.

Role-Play

Role play is acting or re-acting a situation. People play the parts of the participants in the situation. They can either play themselves or others who are involved. When reviewing we use Role-play to replay behaviour in a previous situation or practise behaviour for a future one. This leads not only to experiencing the behaviour but experiencing the thoughts and feelings related to the situation.

Role-play is very useful because it allows the participants to replay their thoughts and feelings about a situation in safety. Often, because it is not the real situation, the feelings are less intense and therefore more manageable. It is possible for the role player to be more aware of what actually happened in the original situation.

Using Role Play to check your perception

By role playing another person in the situation a person's perception can change. For instance, you can replay a row which you had with your partner. You can role play your partner, while someone role plays you. You may then experience some of your partner's feelings and understand why she behaved in the way she did. In the light of this understanding you can practice different ways of dealing with your partner in similar situations. You will be able to see the likely effect of a different approach.

While practising a new approach to discuss a difficult issue with your partner you may discover that you are unable to behave in the way you would ideally like to. If so, you may choose to do some more work to find out what is stopping you changing. You may find it useful to look at your values and beliefs as we mentioned in Chapter 3. Alternatively, you can choose to avoid dealing with the situation until you feel more able to do so. However, having used role play to practise, you may feel more confident to deal with the issue.

Re-viewing procedures

Chrissie used role play with staff in an old people's home to review the admissions procedures. The group took on the roles of different members of staff, a client and her relatives, and a social worker. The group replayed admitting an elderly person to the home to give the relatives a fortnight's holiday break. Having re-acted this situation, everyone was asked to write their thoughts and feelings and then their memories of what actually happened during the role play. This led to discussion about different perceptions of the same situation.

The group realised that their procedures did not help either the client or the relatives to deal with their feelings about the person going into care. They had not realised that the way they carried out the procedure actually added to the stress of the client. The group could now think about the procedures and how they could be changed, to meet the needs of the staff and, more importantly, to meet the needs of the client.

You might think that the same information could have been gathered by simply observing someone being admitted. However, the role play meant that the careworkers actually felt what it was like to be an elderly person coming into the home. They became more committed to changing the procedures with the clients views taken into account. Having experienced the emotions they could more clearly see what changes were necessary to reduce the new client's stress and anxiety.

From this example, you can probably see how role play can easily be used to review procedures to do with people, e.g. a reception procedure in an office block, or a factory, or a hotel, or a G.P.'s surgery, etc., as well as procedures for induction, interviews, people retiring, children starting a new school.

Role play with families

We have also used role play in our family to practise or relive a situation. You can use them to help a child review exactly what happened when he was sent to see the headteacher at school, or any situation where your child is anxious about dealing with another person. Such an anxiety about situations is not just limited to the children in your family. You can practise too.

Another way role play can be used to review is by re-acting childhood situations. Therapists sometimes use this to help people get in touch with emotions that they had as children but buried as they were unable to cope with them at the time. It is very useful to identify situations which led to feelings of shame, guilt, anger or sadness, so that these emotions can be recognised and dealt with. They then have less effect on our reactions to similar situations as an adult. It is important that this work is done with a therapist who is trained to use this technique. Disturbing and painful emotions may be raised if you are looking at emotions which seemed so terrible that you needed to bury them for so long.

The importance of debriefing

All role-plays need time for the participants to be debriefed; given an opportunity to discuss what has happened, to express feelings and to come out of character before moving on to other things. Many years ago we role played a couple being counselled and were not debriefed. The feelings from this remained with us and affected our behaviour for several weeks. This would not have happened if we had been given the opportunity to talk about our feelings at the time.

You may like to think of how you could use role plays to help you review situations at home or at work.

Lists

You probably often use lists to review. At the simplest level we write lists of things to do and check them off when we have done them. Philip has a list which he uses to check out if his room is as tidy as we have all agreed it should be!

Lists are useful because they give a structure to focus our thoughts when we are reviewing. There are all sorts of lists you can use to review. We have shown some below to review:

- a couple's relationship

- a team's effectiveness

- your work and career

- your feelings

From these you will see that you may find it easier to use a list than to review without any structure. The lists simply provide some headings to hang your thoughts on. They also help you compare a review with the last one as you use the same classification of your thoughts.

Re-viewing your relationship with your partner

To review our relationship we used a list we took and adapted from John & Linda Friel's book, "An Adult Child's Guide to what's Normal". We talked about the events of the week so that we both had lists of the "raw material" in our heads. We then each wrote, under the headings, about our relationship during the last week. We used the events of the week we had just talked about as evidence for our conclusions. We then shared and discussed what we had written under each heading, sometimes developing our notes from each other's perspective.

When we came to do the exercise again the following week we compared this week's notes with what we wrote last week. This gave us some measure of how our relationship was devloping and what was happening to us as individuals within the relationship. It also showed repeating patterns. Here is the list we used, followed by some examples of Richard's notes for each heading one week.

Boundaries -	Physical
	Intellectual
	Emotional
	Sexual
	Social
	Time
	Money
Feelings	
Respect	
Love	
Rights and responsibilities	
Beliefs	
Actions	
Decisions	
Power	
Paradoxes	

Richard's notes

Boundaries

Did quite well with "time" when on my own on Wednesday and Thursday - I did practical things, but forgot the washing.

Aware of "physical" boundaries this week - hugging Philip - today I offered and he accepted, rather than me just giving a hug.

"Emotional" still weak. Wanting to give mine to Chrissie - yelling and jumping about on Thursday - she wouldn't take my anger and maintained her boundaries. Leaving room and coming back may be useful.

"Intellectual" - did want to take over from Chrissie when we were writing letters yesterday. I think we sorted it out quickly though.

Feelings

We've both been quite good at dealing with feelings this week - children's letters, going to school, crying incident.

Learned about sulking in the snow.

Anger sometimes expressed inappropriately - jumping about! - but am more aware this week.

Respect

Not showing respect when I take over, nor when I talk incessantly about the training day, nor when I don't listen, nor when I indulge in my feelings at the expense of Chrissie's, but Chrissie protected her boundaries well and so we managed.

Respect for self more this week because we've done our own things as well.

Love

A lot this week, arguments - yes but they have made us more free to love.

Still judging of other people - Monday's meeting.

Rights and responsibilities (Links closely with "Boundaries")

I was better with Philip - swimming on Wednesday.

Have shared responsibility successfully for the writing.

Beliefs

The book is good - it will be published.

We are a good team

Actions

Did what we said we would this week - reviewed, worked, stuck to plan with John, sorted out the children.

Have had time alone, and have read and looked at John Bradshaw's work again.

Haven't meditated daily though - need to think about routine.

Decisions

Still tend to give these to Chrissie - have been aware of it this week, and have said what I think and then asked Chrissie for her view.

Power

All of the stuff about controlling Chrissie on Thursday - I still do it but we sort it out earlier than we used to - we debriefed about last night's meeting better than last week.

Paradoxes

Like having Philip here v. more time when he's not.

Write to the children v. not feeling the pain.

Express feelings to Chrissie (badly) and risk it v. saying it's o.k., knowing that it will pass soon but that I shall be withdrawn.

You may like to try to use this list to review your relationship with your partner. You may like to think of other headings which you might find more useful for you at the moment.

Re-viewing your team's effectiveness

Here is an example of a review list for team development. It was taken from "50 Activities for Teambuilding" by Mike Woodcock, and we have included the instructions for using it.

Purpose

- To help team effectiveness by reviewing performance.

Method

1. The facilitator explains that this is a way of improving team functioning and that if it is to work it demands openness, honesty and a certain amount of risk-taking.

2. Each participant rates team performance against the following headings:

Objectivity	Leadership
Information	Openness
Organisation	Support
Decision-making	Use of time
Participation	Climate

3. The team tries as far as possible to reach a consensus rating which reflects the view of the team.

4. The process can be repeated after further meetings or tasks.

Notes and variations

1. The activity is most useful when used repeatedly.

2. The team can consider the appropriateness of the headings and if desired make changes.

Making your own list

Lists like this are found in management development books. You could simply use the chapter headings from such books as a list for a team to work with. Your team can easily make up its own list. This will probably be even more useful as it will be based on your own values, and team purpose, and will be set in the context of your own organisation's culture.

Re-viewing your work and career

We have used lists to help people change career, perhaps following redundancy or during major company reorganisations. Here is a list and instructions taken from Gill Edwards' book, "Stepping into the Magic". You might like to use it to help you think about your work.

---

1. What do you enjoy? Tick whichever apply from the list below. Give two ticks to any items which are a high priority for you (Feel free to add your own ideas.)

Being creative/innovative ✓
Coming up with new ideas ✓
Meeting new people ✓
Working as part of a team
Being independent ✓
Having to make quick decisions
Having deadlines to meet
Regular, guaranteed income ✓
Research/statistics
Managing/leading others
Having a finished product
Being outdoors/in nature ✓
Travelling ✓

Having an office to go to
Getting the details right
Putting ideas on paper
Working on projects
Working at home
Keeping accounts
Marketing/selling
Money management
Healing
Working with animals ✓
Working with plants ✓
Having a steady income ✓
Being physically active ✓

Taking risks
Singing/dancing/theatre ✓
Using your imagination ✓
Speaking on telephone ✓
Fundraising
Making/building things
Working with mass media
Working on computers
Putting ideas into practice
Inspiring people
Having a business partner(s)
Creating a vision of the future ✓
Helping people one-to-one
Reaching large numbers of
  people
Writing ✓
Teaching
Negotiating
Feeling challenged
Working with people in need
New age ideas
Living in city
Living in countryside ✓

Inner work/meditation
Arts and crafts
Working with your hands
Helping people find solutions
Committee work
Co-ordinating groups
Simplifying complex data
Doing something new ✓
Reading ✓
Having an impact on
institutions
Problem solving
Lots of variety ✓
Lots of free time
Working with children ✓
Working regular hours ✓
Working flexible hours
Caring for others ✓
Being playful ✓
Networking
Busy, hectic workplace
Working in peace and quiet
Running your own business

2. Does your current job offer the opportunities, challenges, and working environment that you have ticked? Could you shift the emphasis in your current job so that it does offer what you want? Or do you need to change your line of work? (Don't assume that you're in the wrong job because you have no like-minded people around you. Your task might be as a Lightkeeper in the company or institution, if that is a role you enjoy.)

3. If you could do anything you wanted, without any financial worries, what would you do? What would your ideal lifestyle be? How could you move towards this lifestyle now?

4. What does success mean to you? (Try to ignore what it means to other people. Ask yourself what it means to you.)

Again, when thinking about a change in work or career, we have found it most useful to help people write their own lists under broad headings. These lists have often included values, skills, interests, experiences, needs, wants, beliefs, aptitudes, preferences. The same skills can be used for different jobs in different types of organisation, so it is important to include values on these lists, e.g. a social worker and a salesman use similar skills but may be working from different value bases, in different organisational cultures.

Re-viewing your feelings

You may find this list of feelings useful when re-viewing as you can check which feelings you've had during the week and when. This will make you more conscious of your feelings, and show you some patterns, e.g. you may notice that you hardly ever experience joy.

Feelings

Angry	Brave
Depressed	Hurt
Aggressive	Guilty
Anxious	Empty
Enthusiastic	Impulsive
Helpless	Inferior
Self conscious	Sensual
Powerful	Trusting
Stressed	Successful
Happy	Joyful
Destructive	Afraid

A Basket Of Goodies

Excited	Hate
Frustrated	Self-pitying
Passionate	Loving
Bored	Vulnerable
Cowardly	Lonely
Compassionate	Creative
Sad	Ashamed
Embarrassed	Depressed
Aggressive	Anxious
Empty	Enthusiastic

Add any others you think of

You might like to try to use any one of these lists which seem appropriate for you at the moment. If we haven't included a list which you think would be helpful try making up a list of your own.

- - - - -

We hope that you find this basket of goodies useful to dip into when you are stuck or need a creative way to review.

CHAPTER TEN

CHANGING YOUR VIEW OF THE WORLD

This book has been about the Wisborough process. A process to re-view and develop. To re-view means to look at again, to see with different eyes, to have a different perspective, to change your view of the world. Have you ever gone back to a place you knew well as a child? Perhaps you visited the school you went to when you were five. Were you surprised by how small it all seemed? Did you remember things which seemed very large and important then, only to find that they now seemed tiny and insignificant? The facts are the same, the building is the same one it was before. All that has changed is your perspective. This is what we often discover when we re-view.

While we maintain our current view of the world, we maintain our beliefs about how we should live our lives. We set our limits, and our choices within these beliefs. We carry on behaving in the same way as always, thinking the usual things, feeling the habitual emotions, as we continue our life along the same tracks. The purpose of reviewing, for us, is to be able to change our view of the world so that we can open up the possibilities and have a whole new range of choices.

Risk Is The Toll For Leaving The Land
of Predictable Mediocrity

It is difficult to give up our old views when we think that we are managing our lives reasonably well. You have to be incredibly brave to take the risk of trying to change something which is reasonably acceptable, just because you think, (but don't know for sure) that it could be better. However, our experience has shown us that raising our consciousness of ourselves and the world around us is worth the risk.

Dennis Potter (the playwright) gave an interview on television when he had discovered that he was shortly to die from cancer. He said that he now looked at the world differently. He was able to enjoy every moment because he was fully conscious of living every moment. He talked about the tree which was blossoming in his garden. He said that he knew it had blossomed every year but now he noticed that it was "the whitest, frothiest, blossomiest blossom ever".

We would like to live our lives with this level of consciousness. We don't want to find that at the end of our lives, we have simply been passing the time away. Wisboroughs help us have this consciousness and encourage us to take the risks.

Rex had recently been made redundant. He had worked for a company for a long time. He had been unhappy for the last few years as the company changed. He had carried on working there, working hard but disliking every day.

He said that if he had known three years ago that it would all end this way, he would probably have been brave enough to choose to leave the company at that time. Instead he wasted three years of his life being unhappy. It was difficult for him to change his view of the world while his world only became worse gradually. He accepted more and more unhappiness because it came to him slowly. He didn't realise how unhappy he had become until he left.

It is like the story of the frog in a pan of water. If the water is gradually heated the frog will slowly boil to death. If the frog is put straight into hot water it will leap out and save itself.

It is difficult to be sufficiently aware of what is happening to you if the changes around you are very gradual.

Dramatic changes

Sometimes you have sudden changes of lifestyle thrust upon you. If your wife leaves you, if you lose your job, if you have to move to another country, or, like Dennis Potter, you suddenly discover that you are about to die, you start to re-view.

When something dramatic does happen to you, you see your world in a completely different way. It is an opportunity to totally reframe, review and take a different course. If we discover that we are going to die soon, we may reframe so that we are conscious of how we use every minute. Previously we probably viewed life as a routine to go through without thinking.

You might like to think now, how you have used the last few days. Have you spent the time the way you would most like to? If not, why not? How might you begin to use your time differently?

Some people handle dramatic change by choosing not to review. They try to pretend that nothing has changed. They are too afraid. You can probably think of someone who did not tell anyone that his partner had left him, or did not tell his wife that he had lost his job. Sometimes Mom tries to protect everyone by not telling Dad that a child is on drugs, or not going to school.

Re-framing

If nothing dramatic is happening in your life, but you think it might be a good idea to re-view, you have to make a conscious decision to review your world and make the most of the life you have. To change your view of the world you can Re-frame. When we Re-frame we literally put our picture of the world into a new frame, so that it looks different.

If you have never seen the difference that another frame makes to a picture you might like to try this exercise.

Experiment by taking a picture, perhaps cut out of a magazine, and put various coloured frames around it. These might be cut from coloured paper. Try a variety of sizes of frames as well.

We recently re-framed a photograph of some flowers and we were surprised at the difference made by the colour of the border. The picture looked less dramatic, and more gentle with a cream border, rather than a white one. A new frame brought out other colours from the picture so that our attention was drawn to other things.

Once we see different things in our world, we have different choices. Re-framing gives us a different focus.

We use Re-framing as a technique because it changes our perspective and our perceptions of ourselves, situations and other people. If you have a counsellor or therapist you may be used to doing this. Most of us rarely try to turn something upside down by ourselves. You can Re-frame on your own, but it is also very useful to work with a group to look at a particular issue or problem.

The helicopter view

There are several ways of Re-framing. The most common one is to try to view the situation in a broader context, i.e. to take an overview as if we are viewing it from above in a helicopter. So, instead of being totally caught up in the detail of what is happening, we put the situation into a much broader frame. This stops us looking so closely at minute details of arrangements, activities, etc. and makes us look at the situation as a whole. We often go back to first principles at this stage, e.g.

- what do we actually want to achieve?

- what is the really important outcome for us?

- what is our real business?

- what is the purpose of the exercise?

When you are at work, do you sometimes find yourself spending more time scoring points off another person than thinking about the real purpose of your job? Perhaps you find yourself continually defending yourself from someone's jibes, rather than working out solutions to the work problem. If so, reframing by stopping to think, "what do I want to achieve?" or "what are we trying to do here?" may help you get back on track.

When talking about Re-framing with a friend of ours called Stephen, he was reminded that he had recently spent twenty minutes getting a saucepan spotlessly clean and then suddenly realised that he had the whole house to clean and tidy before his guests arrived in two hours time. He had forgotten that what he was really trying to achieve was a reasonably clean and tidy house in a few hours. He hadn't taken a helicopter view.

Richard recently worked with a small company which had a number of shops selling a variety of leisure goods. The variety of stock had grown over the years without any conscious planning. The business was making money but no-one was particularly excited by the work.

Bruce, the Managing Director, realised, after quite a lot of discussion, what he was actually in business for and what sort of business he wanted. He had to stop and think. He wanted what he considered to be an "ethical family business". What did he mean by ethical? It included involving the workforce in major decisions, in being a good employer and a model retailer. It also included selling products which were socially acceptable for families.

So, Bruce stopped selling shotguns, and knives. He started involving staff in decision-making and became what he considered to be a model retailer. He had Re-framed by asking himself what his real business was, what he wanted it to be, and why he was in business.

The third corner

Alistair Mant in his book, "The Leaders we Deserve", refers to the third corner. In most relationships there are only two corners. Alistair Mant suggests that we should also think about the third corner, i.e. the product or the purpose of the relationship. He identifies two corner relationships where the participants spend most of their energies competing to survive. When the third corner is identified the participants become aware of what is happening in that corner, what is happening to the product or service, i.e. is the product being produced on time, to the right standard, etc. The third corner then becomes more important. It is the purpose of the relationship.

When we have found ourselves being sucked into other people's games and our emotions have taken over we have found it useful to remember what we wanted the outcome of the discussion to be, i.e. what is the third corner, the purpose. We then keep ourselves focussed on this and we can bring the games to a halt.

Chrissie discovered, when trying to sort out problems about Philip's holidays with her ex-husband, that she was often drawn into wanting to fight. She found that she had to stop and think about what she was really trying to achieve to meet Philip's needs. Originally Chrissie found herself wasting a lot of time and energy fighting about words.

By focussing on the important outcomes, she was able to simply note the words, stay with her emotions and be much more business-like in her dealings with her ex-husband. These games could not continue, as she became more able to resist her own emotional hooks.

Life is cyclical

Another way of enlarging the frame is to realise that the present is only a transitory moment in time. Or, to put it another way, everything is part of a cycle and nothing stays the same forever. This is true for things that make us happy as well as the events that make us sad. By Re-framing we realise the importance of catching the joy of the moment and we realise that the sadness of the moment will pass.

Turning it upside down

Turning it upside down is a way of Re-framing which literally turns everything around, so that we make all the negatives positives and all the positives negative. Instead of being disappointed and saying a recipe isn't right because you had to replace an ingredient for one you didn't have in the cupboard, you can see the recipe as a <u>new</u> recipe with different ingredients and be pleased with it.

If we think we really want something, we can decide to give it away and see what happens. This instantly gives us freedom from wanting to own it. We can begin to think differently about it. Re-framing is about changing or removing the constraints that we put on our thoughts. Therefore, giving away something that we really want to keep releases us from those constraints and allows us the freedom to think more creatively.

For instance, if you are in a relationship where you believe that you need the other person to stay with you, you will spend a lot of time and energy trying to keep him. You will probably try to please him, act out and try to be what he wants, rather than simply be yourself.

If you, instead, decide that you don't need him to stay for you to be alright, you no longer have to behave in this way. You are then free to be yourself and the relationship is more likely to succeed because the other person is less likely to feel trapped by you.

By releasing the trap for the other person you have released your own trap. In other words, by giving a person back to themselves, and no longer trying to own something we think we desperately wanted to own, we are more likely to keep a healthy relationship. We are giving the other person a choice. We are no longer forcing our choice upon them.

Stepping into someone's shoes

Another way of Re-framing is to stop thinking about ourselves and to try to understand why the other person in behaving in a particular way. If we can understand why someone is doing something it often helps us take a different approach. For instance, you might realise that someone isn't being aggressive towards you because they hate you but rather, because they are afraid or upset. Their aggressive behaviour may have nothing to do with you. You can then look at the situation more objectively.

When Chrissie started running courses for managers she worked out how to deal with aggressive participants in a group. She imagined their aggression being thrown at her, but instead of it landing on her and staying in her stomach, she saw it landing on the floor in front of her. She could then sift it and see what belonged to her and what belonged elsewhere, i.e. what had she contributed towards this person feeling angry and what had been contributed by himself, his wife, his children, his boss, colleagues, etc.

If we stop trying to protect ourselves and start to wonder why the other person is finding it necessary to protect himself, we can start to view things from his perspective instead of ours. This encourages us to try to resolve issues rather than fight.

As you can probably see, this new frame is useful when you feel the need to defend yourself by attacking or withdrawing. Re-framing leads you to care about the other person rather than defend yourself and dismiss him. This may sound difficult or you may feel that it is too risky not to defend yourself. If so, it is best to practise in reasonably safe situations until you are confident that Re-framing can work. You might like to think of examples of safe situations where you could practise Re-framing. For instance, you may not be able to practise when your boss is shouting at you across the room, but you think you could when your partner is behaving in a similar fashion at home.

Another way of stepping into someone's shoes, which we have used, is to literally go and sit in their seat when they have gone. At the end of the day when the group has gone home, we sometimes sit in each person's chair in turn and say what we thought that person would say about the day. We often gain insights about someone's views by doing this. You can probably see, from the last chapter, the similarities with this and role-plays.

Exploring How Our Thoughts and Feelings Affect Our Behaviour

You have seen how much your feelings affect your behaviour. If you can identify how your thoughts lead to your feelings, you can then modify your behaviour by changing your thoughts. A process which will help you to do this is Ken & Kate Back's process (from their book "Assertiveness at Work") for dealing with unsound inner dialogue. Since we first came across this idea we have taken it and adapted it to help us Re-frame.

This concept is based on the idea that your thoughts about a situation instantly give you feelings and you react to those feelings by behaving in a particular way. You may feel hurt and therefore behave aggressively, or frightened so that creative thinking is blocked. You may be unaware of your thoughts. You just know that you have a knot in your stomach. This normally happens very quickly, and you seem to have no control over it.

To gain some control you need to slow down the process and intervene in the thoughts before they can be translated into negative feelings and so affect your behaviour. You cannot totally change your feelings or behaviour but you can modify them so that panic can become concern, fury can become frustration, and fear can become an appropriate awareness of the dangers.

The process will give you an opportunity to take time to identify your thoughts, and check out their origins and validity in the current situation. You can then explore ways of changing those thoughts to more appropriate ones. This will have an effect on your feelings and so allow you to choose how you want to behave.

We have outlined below some thoughts, some feelings which might come as a result of these thoughts and some behaviours which might be your reaction to those feelings.

THOUGHTS > FEELINGS > BEHAVIOUR

THOUGHTS	FEELINGS	BEHAVIOUR
A memory	Anxiety	Fight or flight
A negative image	Panic	Aggressive/passive
A positive belief	Joy	Assertive

Using Your Thoughts and Feelings to Change Your Behaviour

First, you need to identify your current thoughts. You may find the following headings useful: Memory, Image, Rights, Obligations, Anticipated behaviour and consequences.

You now need to identify the feelings you have as a result of your thoughts. You can now challenge your thoughts and modify your feelings so that finally, you can work out what you are able to do.

Memory

Your memory of similar situations or events will lead you to particular feelings about a future event. If you have positive memories you will have positive feelings, if negative thoughts about a past experience you will experience negative feelings. Unfortunately memory is very selective. We often only remember specific incidents during the event, we ignore all the other evidence, or we exagerate and see everything in black and white. We forget all the grey areas.

Your positive or negative feelings will lead you to behave in an habitual way in the coming situation. If you can explore your memories of the previous event you can modify your feelings. You can also decide to choose your behaviour, rather than simply react and fall into your usual pattern of behaviour.

Image

We often have an image of how we like to be seen in situations and become anxious if we think that we shall not be seen in this way. These images have been impressed upon us since child-hood, e.g. how you are supposed to behave as a woman, what you are supposed to look like, what your mother's view is of you, the label you were given at school or at home, how successful you should be by the time you're thirty.

If you explore some of these thoughts you may discover that you do not need to keep these images, and that nothing terrible will happen to you if people see you differently. You may discover that you like yourself even if you are different from the way your friends think you should be. As soon as you begin to explore your ideas about the images you try to maintain and the reasons behind your beliefs, your feelings will be altered and you will be free to change your behaviour if you want to.

Rights

Your beliefs about your rights and other people's rights in a situation will also affect your feelings and behaviour. Your feelings about going to a meeting will probably be negative if you believe that you do not have the right to say no, and you know that you are going to be asked to do something you don't really want to do. In the same way, if you believe that you are not allowed to make mistakes, you will always be worrying about getting things right or how you can be sure that you will not be found out.

Again your beliefs about rights have been with you a long time and are probably the most difficult to change. So, it is very useful to ask yourself "why..." and "what if..." to try to establish a clearer picture of your rights.

We often don't know when we are reacting to beliefs about our rights. If you find yourself in a situation where you don't feel good about yourself it may mean that someone is taking away a right which you thought you had. Here is a simple example of this. You believe that you have the right to be called by your name and your boss calls you "dear" or a nickname instead. You often feel irritated at work. It may be because your right to be called by your name has been taken away. It is worth checking out your beliefs about your rights in a situation when you find your emotions taking over.

Obligations

We have all been brought up with certain obligations; the "shoulds" and "oughts" which we carry with us. These link very closely with our image of ourselves and our beliefs about rights. How often do you do something because you think you should, rather than because you want to or could. A way to help us check out our "shoulds" and "oughts" is to change the word "should" or "ought" into "could", e.g. "I should take Mary to the shops today" becomes "I could take Mary to the shops today". This instantly gives us a choice and changes our emotions. It also helps us examine our real feelings about doing something.

Once we have a choice the feeling of being driven and therefore behaving with bad grace is less likely. We may still think that it is a good idea to take Mary to the shops but we don't have to do it today. Giving ourselves some choices, changes our feelings about ourselves, the situation and the people involved. We feel more in control of ourselves, less martyred or stressed and can then behave more positively.

Anticipated behaviour and consequences

When it comes to anticipating our behaviour and its consequences our imagination begins to work overtime. This is when our inner chatterbox takes over with all its negative contributions to our thoughts. This is when I <u>know</u> that I am going to do something awful and look silly, this is when I <u>know</u> that I will be unable to answer anyone's questions and they will not offer me the job, this is when I <u>know</u> that I shall miss the goal and will not get a place in the team.

Actually, this is when you <u>know</u> you need to check out the probability that you will behave in a particular way and the likelihood of the result you are forecasting really happening. You also need to question how much it really matters if your worst fears do materialise.

You can then begin to work out realistic strategies for dealing with realistic possibilities arising during the situation. For instance, you no longer have to suspect that everyone will disagree with your idea (thought). You no longer have to be afraid (feeling). You no longer have to try to bulldoze your proposal through the meeting (behaviour). Instead you can plan for the meeting, be well informed, identify people who are likely to support you, identify what people may dislike about your proposal and how its advantages outweigh its disadvantages.

What can you do?

You might like to use this process for yourself now. Use the following questions to review your thoughts and feelings about a situation which you know is coming soon and which you would like to plan for now. This might be easier than waiting until you are in a crisis and your feelings have taken over. It will give you time to practise in a safe setting.

You can use these questions if you are feeling anxious about:

- talking a problem over with your partner,

- confronting your son about his behaviour at school,

- a presentation you have to give at work,

- an interview you have next week,

- talking to your neighbour about parking in your place, etc.

Re-framing questions

Memory

What is your memory of a similar situation?
How does this make you feel about the new situation?
How do these feelings affect your behaviour?
Is this memory really relevant to the new situation? What are the similarities and differences?
Was it really that bad/good? Can you rate it on a scale of one to ten?
What evidence supports your thoughts?
Is there any evidence which contradicts your thoughts? What is it?
What have you left out?
How much might you have exaggerated?
What is your memory now of the situation?

Image

What is the image you are trying to project in this situation?
How does this make you feel about the situation?

How do these feelings affect your behaviour?
Where does this image come from?
Why is it important to you?
Is the image still appropriate?
What would happen if you don't maintain the image?
Check out your beliefs about other specific images. How realistic are they for you now?
What do you now think about your image in this situation?

Rights

What are your beliefs about your rights in this situation?
What are your beliefs about other people's rights?
Do you believe some of your rights have been transgressed? If so, which ones?
Do you believe you have transgressed someone's rights? If so, which ones?
How does this make you feel about the situation?
How do these feelings affect your behaviour?
Where do these beliefs about rights come from?
Why do you think they are appropriate?
What do you now think about rights in this situation?

Obligations

What do you believe you "should" or "ought" to do in this situation?
How does this make you feel about the situation?
How do these feelings affect your behaviour?
Why do you believe you have these obligations?
Where do they come from?
Are they appropriate to this situation?
What would happen if you didn't meet them?
What would happen if you change "should" to "could"?

What do you now believe you "should" or "ought" to do in this situation?

Anticipated behaviour and consequences
What do you believe is likely to happen?
How does this make you feel about the situation?
How do these feelings affect your behaviour?
What is the chance of this actually happening?
How much might you have exaggerated or catastrophised?
Has your chatterbox taken you into a negative spiral of self doubt?
Does it really matter if your fears come true?
Can you now describe your more realistic picture of what might happen?

Having worked through these questions your feelings about the situation have probably been modified. You can now practically plan what you want to do in the situation, rather than be driven by your feelings. So, with the information gained from your answers, think what you can now realistically do in the situation.

This technique for re-framing will give you the opportunity to choose appropriate behaviour for a particular situation. You will not simply repeat old patterns of behaviour or react to your feelings. By exploring your thoughts and their effect on your feelings you can slow down the process and decide how you want to behave in the circumstances.

Taking All This Further

Hopefully you have been able to see how this technique of interrupting and challenging the thoughts - feelings - behaviour patterns can be used to help in everyday situations. For longer term personal development you can use the techniques in this book to free yourself from the frame you have constructed. This frame can become a cage or a trap from which we think we cannot escape. We set our own limitations constantly. Wisboroughs change the boundaries of the frame so that it may even be possible to remove them completely. We have to be very brave to work with that level of freedom.

If we want to do this, we have to let go and allow ourselves to see the world differently. You can only do this if you let yourself doubt, and question concepts and facts of which you were previously sure.

We often take our view of the world completely for granted. Earlier in the book we looked at the values and beliefs you use to help you maintain your view of the world. Some people are unaware of the fundamental belief system, upon which they base their view of the world. However, they are using this belief system to make the decisions which affect the way they live their lives. Wisboroughs encourage you to be aware of your fundamental beliefs and be courageous enough to question them.

People often find the idea of such doubt too difficult and prefer to maintain their safe view. You can't let your safe view go until you are ready to. You need to choose your own time.

Letting Go

Here is a list. You may be holding on to beliefs about any of these. If you can empty yourself of old thought patterns, you can allow in others. While you are full up, nothing new can be seen or felt. You might like to explore your beliefs about them and see what you can let go.

Memories of important events	Gender
Doubt	War
Rules & constraints	Aggression
Birth	Discipline
Behaviour	Feelings
Power	Freedom
Negative feelings	Positive feelings
The results	The process
Your image	Your true self
Your chatterbox	Your own thoughts
Logic	Intuition
Rights	Responsibilities
The Conscious	The Unconscious
Creativity	Self worth
Children	Parents
Marriage	Divorce
Managers	Work
God	Sex
Death	Reality
Staircases	Houses
Fear	Love

You may find some of the Re-framing questions help your exploration.

You may think that our list is strange. You are probably right. The point is that we have beliefs about everything and we all have a list. What we are trying to do when we re-view, if we want to grow, is keep adding new thoughts to the list and letting old, no longer needed, beliefs go from it.

Whatever we are holding on to, we can explore and see what would happen if we let it go. We have the opportunity to see the world differently if we continually ask questions and become fully conscious of our world. America would never have been discovered by Europeans if they had continued to believe that the world was flat.

By questioning all our beliefs we can ultimately remove our frame completely. What we then see is what our innermost soul sees. This view is unsullied by our beliefs, values and feelings of self worth. We will see things as they are to us. We will be in touch with the world. We will no longer be separated by our beliefs, values and feelings of self worth. Our perception will be clear. The barriers will be removed.

Not only will my soul be able to see but you will be able to see my soul.

Another way of exploring this idea is to think about where you are hanging your picture. If you hang it on a wall, then the wall frames it. It becomes part of the wall, part of the system that it hangs in. You could hang it in the garden or put it in the centre of a town. In each it will be part of a different system. It becomes part of the garden or the town. It will have an effect upon the way the garden or the town looks, and feels. On a larger scale, it might be that we see our picture framed only by the world, or perhaps by the universe.

Which system frames your view of reality?

The purpose of this book has been to help you re-view so that you can re-frame your picture of the world, become aware of the choices and develop in the direction you wish to take. We hope that you enjoy the journey.